How to Invest in Strategic Metals

How to Invest in Strategic Metals

Bohdan Szuprowicz

St. Martin's Press   New York

Copyright © 1982 by Bohdan Szuprowicz
All rights reserved. For information, write:
St. Martin's Press, Inc., 175 Fifth Avenue, New York, N.Y. 10010.
Manufactured in the United States of America

Library of Congress Cataloging in Publication Data

Szuprowicz, Bohdan O., 1931–
  How to invest in strategic metals.
    1. Metal trade—Finance. 2. Strategic materials.
I. Title.
HD9506.A2S98   332.63   81-21476
ISBN 0-312-39575-2   AACR2

Design by Kingsley Parker

10 9 8 7 6 5 4 3 2 1

First Edition

To Majusia,
the most critical of my editors, and wife

contents

	Preface	ix
	Introduction: The Resources War	xi

1. What You Need to Know about Strategic Metals

1.	"Strategics": Some High-Tech Stories	3
2.	"The Gold of the 1980s"?	18
3.	Criticality: Availability	28
4.	Criticality: Substitutability	41
5.	What about Scrap Recycling?	49
6.	Stockpiles of Strategic Metals	54
7.	Who Trades in Strategic Metals?	58
8.	Where to Find Strategic Metals Prices	71
9.	The Laws That Affect Strategic Metals Trade and Use	80

2. Mechanics of Strategic Metals Trading

10.	How to Buy Strategic Metals	88
11.	Which Documents Are Important?	112
12.	When to Sell Strategic Metals	121

3. Investment Alternatives to Direct Ownership of Strategic Metals

13.	How about a Strategic Metals Investment Fund?	134
14.	Which Company Stocks Are Strategic Metals Investments?	153

4. Where to Get More Information on Strategic Metals

15.	Sources	162
	Index	219

Preface

Strategic metals present one of the most exciting investment opportunities for the rest of this century. They are hard assets that are crucial to national defense and high technology industries, and many are much rarer than gold. Their limited supplies are often threatened by unrest in politically unstable countries, and their prices can increase several times within a very short time.

During 1980, strategic metals became a new investment vehicle for governments, corporations, institutions, and private investors. As a tangible and useful asset they are a superb inflation hedge while their price performance offers unusual speculation and trading opportunities as well.

Investor interest in strategic metals is growing rapidly in North America and the British Isles. In other countries like Germany, Switzerland, and Japan there is mounting awareness of the new opportunities. This may develop into a global upsurge of demand for the relatively limited supplies of strategic metals and a dramatic escalation of their prices well above the inflation levels or interest returns on other forms of investment.

But whereas strategic metals offer unusual investment opportunities there are also a number of pitfalls that a newcomer must be aware of before plunging into this game. Exciting and promising as it is strategic metals investment is not for the uninformed or those unwilling to accept the realities of this industry.

Because strategic metals are a new investment vehicle there is relatively little information available as yet to the average investor

HOW TO INVEST IN STRATEGIC METALS

about their performance. Yet the key to success in this game is the understanding of the limits of criticality of strategic metals as their supplies and prices change due to geopolitical shifts in the world. This book is designed to lay bare all the facts and shatter any illusions about strategic metals investment. It has been written with the average investor in mind, but brokers, dealers, traders, and corporate executives should find it equally useful because it describes a new and recent development on the investment scene that has hitherto gone almost undocumented.

There are four basic sections in the book. The first section defines strategic metals, their most critical applications, their availability, and the limits beyond which substitution comes into play. The second part describes the process of investing in physical strategic metals and the mechanics of buying and selling decisions that must be made. The third section goes into alternative investment opportunities such as strategic metals mutual funds, commodity pools, inventories, stockpiles, and recycling operations. The last section may turn out to be the most valuable to the serious investor because it identifies most of the sources of strategic metals information throughout the world that will keep you abreast of developments affecting your investments.

It is now up to you. If you read this book carefully you will at least have no excuse for being taken, and you may even come out well ahead with a strategic metals stockpile of your very own.

Bohdan O. Szuprowicz
North Bergen, New Jersey, May 1982

Introduction
The Resources War

The struggle for resources is as old as life itself. All species of plants and animals and all races, nationalities, and tribes of man have been at it since time immemorial. But now there are so many people on this planet and we are so adept in setting up all sorts of borders and restrictions that we can no longer freely move from one green pasture to another once we deplete its resources.

Instead we move commodities from those who have them to those who need them, and we do it according to another set of very smart rules designed for people to exploit other people in some tolerable manner. But the golden rule of these transactions is increasingly becoming that "he who has the gold makes the rules."

That's what the Arabs did with oil when they created the OPEC cartel. However, the Arabs were not the first and will probably not be the last at this game. Nazi Germany had similar ambitions for their One-Thousand-Year Reich. Imperial Japan called it the "Asian Co-Prosperity Sphere." The Bolsheviks had set up communist Soviet state monopolies and had been getting away with it for over sixty years. Now there is talk of OMEC, meaning Organization of Minerals Exporting Countries. Other "price stabilization" schemes for specific metals and minerals are also in the works.

Before World War I the United States was the undisputed leader in oil and minerals production. When American oil companies suddenly raised the price of oil the European importing countries screamed with indignation but paid the price because there were few alternative sources. Fortunately they were not too dependent on oil at that time, so they went on burning coal, wood, and peat. But the whole world learned a lesson it never forgot.

Those were the good old days. Life was simple. Technology was iron and steel, and coal fueled the railways. Airplanes were made of wood and bicycle chains. Armies moved on horseback frightening each other with sabers and big bangs of gunpowder. More often than not they waited out the night or bad weather before they could take decisive action. Gorgeous blondes gathering intelligence consorted with the generals, and aluminum was just a laboratory curiosity.

Today thousands of satellites circle the globe day and night peering through darkness and clouds, sensing movements of nuclear submarines under the oceans from hundreds of miles above the earth and relaying that information with incredible precision to computers thousands of miles away. Missiles and rockets with nuclear warheads are poised ready for launching at a moment's notice, capable of obliterating whole cities within minutes. Masses of people fly all over the world in supersonic aircraft, and global communications are instantaneous. Now the availability of even little known rhodium may be a question of national survival.

Those tremendous advances in mankind's science and technology came about rapidly as a result of extensive research into the properties of various minor metals and their alloys. The unique characteristics of these metals made it all possible. The industrialized countries of the North, capitalist and communist alike, have the skills and the capital to make such discoveries and build the equipment. But the developing countries of the South are now finding out that they possess the mineral resources from which many critical metals originate, and they also want a piece of the action and the political power that it entails.

To make matters a little more interesting, the rich developed countries have often depleted their own resources and restricted further development as a result of environmental regulation. They are now increasingly dependent on the Third World for supplies of many of the most critical metals. The Third World is increasingly aware of the situation. Add to this the East-West conflict, and the stage is set for a global struggle of unparalleled proportions. The resources war is on whether we like it or not.

part 1
What You Need to Know about Strategic Metals

chapter 1
"Strategics": Some High-Tech Stories

Strictly speaking, "strategic" pertains to war and the military-industrial complex. Besides the basic metals such as iron and steel, copper, aluminum, nickel, lead, tin, and zinc, most so-called minor metals are either critical or very useful and important in the manufacture of military weapons and equipment. These metals also happen to be quite critical in continuing the development of high technology industries and the economy as a whole.

Rather than presenting a boring list of metals with their corresponding strategic applications this chapter introduces them through a series of articles about high technology industries and weapons systems. The critical roles played in most of these industries by specific minor metals are pointed out and reasons for criticality of many are explained. For simplicity rather than for any scientific reason we call all metals discussed in this book strategic whether or not they are in fact used primarily in the military programs or exist in the National Strategic Defense Stockpile.

The Space Wars Are Coming

You've heard of Soviet "killer" satellites, laser guns, and other science fiction energy weapons that vaporize hostile spaceships. Such systems are already taking shape in American and Soviet laboratories in highly classified programs, and those who have a need to know are now trying to figure out what their strategic value will be. One thing is certain, however—that without strategic metals those weapons cannot be built. The Soviet concern about military aspects of the American space shuttle is your best proof that something is afoot.

The space-based laser weapon is the most attractive idea because it can be a satellite "killer" or antisatellite system (ASAT) or an antiballistic missile (ABM) defense system. Whoever sets it up first will be in a position to sense the hot exhaust of a missile being launched and destroy it a few seconds later with a high-energy laser beam. Authorities figure that eighteen such battle stations in orbit can take care of one thousand enemy missiles in twenty minutes and make the present strategic weapons forces useless overnight. You can bet the last ruble in the Soviet Union that they are going to give it a damn good try, because it literally means the domination of the world. It is the ultimate in strategic blackmail.

The so-called "light metals" and "electronic metals" among the strategics are crucial to the development of these space laser weapons systems and various countermeasures to protect them. But the demand for various strategic metals in these programs is only faintly outlined at present. We don't really want a rush into some very scarce metals that come mostly from South Africa or the Soviet Union.

Mirrors, believe it or not, are very important in laser weaponry because it's all done with light. Mirrors mean reflective surfaces and the most reflective metal known is not silver, familiar to you from your household mirror, but rhodium, a platinum group metal that also has the distinction of being the most expensive metal in the world (priced at $600 per troy ounce in mid-1981).

In addition to mirrors used in laser beam generation the laser ABM will require very large computer-controlled mirrors placed on satellite platforms to rapidly deflect laser beams and take care of those missiles that could be launched simultaneously from such diverse places as Siberia, Angola, Vietnam, and Cuba.

By the way, laser weapons do not destroy objects in space by vaporizing them in Buck Rogers style. That takes too much energy and is not really necessary. It is enough to heat the skin of a target in space. It deforms, the structure weakens, and the missile falls apart as useless space debris. But there's the rub. Since

"STRATEGICS": SOME HIGH-TECH STORIES

a laser beam is light, if you can reflect enough of it away from the target you may pass unharmed. If mirrors can direct laser beams they can also save missiles or space installations in the form of reflective coatings.

Some of those space structures are so huge that there probably is not enough rhodium produced to protect all of it anyway. If that interests you as a fundamental reason to bet on a rhodium demand explosion in the future, think about this: There is another potential market in the works that has already been delayed because of a lack of rhodium. But wait till we get into pollution control.

Iridium, another platinum metal, is also vital in space war programs because key laser components can only be manufactured in iridium crucibles. It has something to do with crystal purity and the fact that iridium is the least corrosive metal known to man, despite what you may have been taught about gold and platinum. This means it is also very useful for making super-reliable electrical contacts, as those in space must be. Iridium is also used in making electronic components that are resistant to nuclear explosion effects. Let's make no mistake about that. Sooner or later "accidental" explosions in space will threaten to disable, even before they can start to function, all those good things everybody is trying to put up there at great expense. So some system survivalability must be built in.

Fiber optics within satellites and space battle stations are also important because neither electronic countermeasures nor nuclear explosion effects can interfere with such communication channels. The bonus here also lies in the fact that fiber optics systems cannot be intercepted or tapped by even the smartest KGB counterintelligence experts. The production of fiber optics uses germanium, indium, gallium, and arsenic. More on this when I discuss super-telecommunications.

The space-based laser weapons also need sensors, detectors, and infrared telescopes, and much of that also depends on indium, antimony, and germanium. The power to run all those wonderful gadgets must come from solar systems, and these cannot be built without silicon, gallium, cadmium, tellurium, or selenium.

Last but not least are the "light metals," which are not sensitive to light, heat, or electronic impulses, but are absolutely vital in space structures because of their light weight combined with toughness. Beryllium, magnesium, and titanium and their various alloys are the basics in large aircraft, satellites, and inertial navigation systems.

In case you still think it's all science fiction stuff, be assured that thanks to the discovery of the unusual properties of various strategic and minor metals the basic technology to put up orbital laser battle stations exists in the Soviet Union and the United States right now. The question is who will pay for it and when.

Electronic and Infrared Warfare Everywhere

Conventional armies are also getting more sophisticated in a hurry, creating an immediate demand for some of the same strategic metals space weapons are dependent upon. Radar, you see, is not foolproof. Enemy planes, tanks, and ships can be identified and targeted for destruction, so jamming devices and a whole array of electronic countermeasures (ECM) have been invented to neutralize and deceive radar intelligence. Then electronic counter-countermeasures (ECCM) were developed to take care of that problem. This game could have continued endlessly, but infrared warfare was born, thanks to indium, antimony, and germanium.

Armies of the East, West, and the Third World are now rushing to equip themselves with "fire-and-forget" self-guided weapons that rely on infrared (IR) guidance because it cannot be jammed by electronic countermeasures. Indium antimonide IR sensors and germanium windows and lenses do the trick in heat-seeking missiles. A weapon such as the Sidewinder, let loose in the general direction of a Libyan fighter, follows the hot exhaust of the jet engine and literally disappears up its tailpipe, blowing up the plane in the process. Very effective, and all the air forces want something like it.

Air-to-ground missiles and ground-to-ground weapons can similarly make mincemeat of your tanks, trucks, or ships, even in the dark. Some laser-guided IR missiles are even better. They are now also equipping foot soldiers with shoulder-launched IR missiles. Can you imagine how much indium it will take to equip the four-million-strong Chinese army, for example? And the Chinese have to have it because they're up against the Russians, who are very much in love with all those IR-guided weapons.

"STRATEGICS": SOME HIGH-TECH STORIES

Sensors, Detectors, and Surveillance Technology

All those infrared-guidance weapons depend on sensors made of indium compounds with antimony, tellurium, or selenium as well as germanium and silicon, but sensor use is not limited to military weapons. Other military and civilian uses are growing rapidly, particularly these days when we are bracing ourselves to combat increasing crime and terrorism for the rest of the century.

It all depends on the fact that those indium semiconductors are extremely sensitive to very minute changes of temperature even miles away. And so a kind of infrared TV, called the Forward Looking Infrared (FLIR), was developed that detects and reproduces radiation patterns on a screen even in total darkness or poor weather. FLIR has excellent potential as an antismuggling and surveillance device anywhere in the world.

Fire detection systems and energy loss detectors also use the same sensors, so if we have a few more towering infernos the building codes will have to be further tightened up and the demand for these metals could explode.

Some still secret sensors of very large size are in the works for the purposes of space surveillance. A giant "eye" made up of thousands of silica chips could monitor a tank or a car on the ground. Both sides are also hard at work in getting an infrared array sensor to detect and monitor submarines. There is a slight temperature difference between the wake of a moving submarine and the surrounding water, and the powers think they can pick that up from hundreds of miles in space.

There are many other applications of those wonderful sensors for guidance and control systems in aircraft, missiles, and satellites, and they are also bound to have something to do with the "stealth" bomber plane. That's the one that can make itself invisible to enemy radar by use of special skin coatings laced with fine metal wiring that can be heated under computer control and confuse the radar. Very hush-hush as yet what's in it, but you know better.

However, the detectors that really excite me are the simple thin strips of indium or gold foil that absorb radioactivity. If you wear one of those in your buttonhole and get caught in some nuclear disaster, your contamination level can be checked. Just imagine what a rush there could be on indium if nuclear proliferation causes some nuclear terrorist action in a major city. The survivalists may blow it up out of proportion any day anyway and I can just see the jewelry industry coming out with mushroom-shaped indium or gold brooches. Gold, of course, is just as good but much more expensive; indium is the poor man's radioactivity sensor. Germanium is also used as a gamma radiation detector.

Rockets, Missiles, Ammunition

The common link between those uses of strategic metals is the need for materials that are very strong, light in weight, and can withstand extremely corrosive chemicals like liquid oxygen and hydrogen. It is the space race of the 1950s and 1960s that really started it all in a big way.

Beryllium, cobalt, hafnium, selenium, silicon, and titanium were not in commercial production until the 1940s. The real rush started after the Soviet Sputnik began to orbit the earth in 1957. That's when bismuth, columbium, germanium, tantalum, tellurium, vanadium, and zirconium stopped being just laboratory curiosities.

Missiles are nothing but fuel tanks full of corrosive chemicals, so stainless steels and titanium alloys are particularly important. Rocket engines must operate at very high temperatures and pressures, and the trick is to develop refractory materials that can take the punishment. Metals like cobalt, columbium, nickel, titanium, tungsten, and zirconium are of vital importance.

Ammunition is akin to rockets in its material demands. Shells must contain explosion without changing shape, although corrosion is not as severe a factor as in liquid-fueled rockets. Here the use of antimony, chromium, copper, lead, and zinc is a long-established tradition. In fact, most strategic metals are in use in one ammunition or another, and you can bet that a neutron warhead is a very fine precision engineering product using only the best of strategic metals.

Computers and Semiconductors

Computers and semiconductors are the pillars of the electronics revolution. Semiconductors are the basic elements from which all

"STRATEGICS": SOME HIGH-TECH STORIES

electronic equipment is made. Computers are just semiconductor chips linked together in very clever logical circuits that are indispensible for driving and controlling much of the rest of electronic equipment in the world. Both semiconductors and computers depend on strategic metals and their combinations. Without some strategic metals, such as antimony, gallium, silicon, or rhenium, modern electronics would cease to exist.

During the 1980s the U.S. military electronics market alone is expected to almost quadruple from $20 billion in 1980 to at least $76 billion in 1990, as estimated in current dollars by the Electronic Industries Association. The growth of computers within the military will do even better, increasing sevenfold in general and almost tenfold when it comes to the so-called "embedded" computers that steer and control all those cruise missiles, smart bombs, and guidance systems.

In 1980 the Department of Defense picked up just over 10,000 of those weapons computers for a mere $4 billion. By 1990 they are forecasting a need for 250,000 units worth $38 billion, more than twice the total value of all the strategic metals produced in the world today. This customer will need a lot of semiconductor materials and metals just for the computers, not to mention the sensors, connectors, and structures that come under nonelectronic categories but are also heavy strategic metals consumers.

And what do you think the Russians will do? Why, they will have to match all this military electronic sophistication if they have to lie, steal, and take potatoes away from the mouths of hungry Ukrainians.

What about germanium, you may ask? Is it not the prime electronic strategic metal that everybody gets excited about? Yes and no. Germanium was big in semiconductor production twenty years ago when the transistor was still king. In 1968 the United States consumed 19,000 kilograms of germanium, but ever since it has been downhill for good old germanium as silicon replaced it. Now germanium is making a comeback in electro-optics. At least 50 percent of all germanium is used in that industry, but its semiconductor heydays are over.

This demonstrates a very important aspect of all high technology industries—the rapid innovation it constantly undergoes. A metal that is critical today is almost discarded as useless a few years later. The demise of germanium also brought along a disaster for indium in electronics, which was used for making alloy connections of germanium semiconductors. Indium consumption in electronics tumbled down from 250,000 troy ounces in 1972 to a low of only 60,000 ounces in 1979. Indium is making a bit of a comeback now, but even the best estimates for its consumption in that market by the year 2000 indicate it will never regain more than half of its consumption levels of 1972 and its market share will continue to fall nevertheless. Did somebody try to sell you indium because of its bright future in electronics? Watch out! It is a has-been in this industry at least.

Tantalum is another strategic metal that also owes much to the electronics industry because capacitors made from this metal are superior to all others. This is particularly true when it comes to cramming components on the dense circuit boards of minicomputers and microprocessors embedded in all those fancy weapons systems. About 70 percent of tantalum use is in electronics such as vital computer systems used in navigational guidance, antisubmarine warfare (ASW), and various radars. When tantalum shot up in price to over $100 per pound in 1980 and supplies became erratic, however, many manufacturers began looking for alternatives, switching to aluminum capacitors without much ado. But the military equipment makers are often locked into use of tantalum by performance specifications, which makes it a truly strategic metal. So it looks like tantalum has a pretty bright future in the electronics world despite recent consumption and price declines.

Then of course there are more advanced semiconductor devices like the "bubble memory," which relies on use of gallium and gadolinium. Miniaturization leads to microelectronic circuits that must also operate with very reliable contacts made possible with iridium, ruthenium, platinum, gold, and silver.

In general electronics consumes the greatest selection of strategic metals and incidentally is the largest industrial user of gold. The important thing to remember is the rapid growth and introduction of electronic devices into all aspects of society to improve productivity. This is possible because electronic components decline about 28 percent in cost every year, chiefly because many strategic metals make it possible. But you've got to run pretty fast to keep track of what's happening in this industry. Always watch

"STRATEGICS": SOME HIGH-TECH STORIES

the Japanese, who want to be the "Numero Uno" in electronics and even computers by the 1990s.

Solar Power Is Very Big Business

The scramble in this game is to produce a solar cell that will convert sunpower directly into electricity at a price competitive with all the conventional fuels. Despite what your local politico may be claiming, the fact is that electric power, even from expensive Arab fuel oils, is still many times cheaper than that produced by solar devices in use today.

But energy costs are creeping up and research into solar cell materials is intensive because the stakes are enormous. The solar cell market is now about $50 million per year, but if a cost-effective solar cell is developed this could explode to an estimated $30 billion per year by the end of the century.

Silicon, selenium, gallium, indium, cadmium, and tellurium in combination with each other and other metals are in the forefront of solar cell research. Cadmium-telluride and gallium-arsenide cells have been in the news recently as solar cell breakthroughs, but their electricity production costs are still far more expensive than oil and gas. However, if a gallium-arsenide cell is developed as a low-cost device, demand for gallium would jump from a few tons in 1990 to 2,000 tons in 2200. One report suggests a price of $850 per kilogram of gallium for that use, which means a market of $17 billion. That is about what all strategic metals that are produced in the world per year are worth today.

Now Titanium Submarines Also

Ships and submarines have traditionally meant steel hulls, and navy ships are reinforced with armor steel that uses a lot of chromium and other ferroalloys to make it tough. Ships also mean a lot of piping for hot water, superheated steam, and all types of corrosive liquids, fuels, and gases, almost like a chemical plant.

The Russians have scored a first in submarines by coming out with titanium hulls instead of steel, which makes their subs run faster and deeper—they can literally run circles around any western submarine. If you have not heard about it yet, it is because the

United States does not even know how to build such a submarine. The Russians did it first because they are also the largest titanium producers in the world, and the performance characteristics of titanium subs are so superior that the United States will have to do it too, to keep even under the oceans.

Six Soviet Alpha-class titanium submarines are being built and launched, each with a displacement of 30,000 tons, almost twice the size of submarines in service today. This uses the equivalent to almost half of all the titanium metals produced annually in the world. The new Soviet subs can develop speeds of up to forty-two knots, which is much faster than U.S. submarines, and they can apparently dive to a depth of eight thousand feet, twice as deep as any western vessel. If undersea nuclear mines and torpedoes exploded near such a titanium submarine, it might survive, while a steel hull would be crushed out of existence. Chances are that the West will also go for titanium subs. One indication is that companies are building additional titanium metal plant capacity while consumption and prices are in decline.

Supertelecommunications

Telecommunications as such is copper wire and cable. Whatever you may have heard about its displacement by fiber optics, it is a long way from that as yet. But telecommunications is also electronics, and you may be surprised to know that within the electronics markets communications is the largest of them all. Computers are growing more rapidly, however, and by the mid-1980s will become the largest electronics industry sector.

What is *exciting* about telecommunications, nevertheless, is the introduction of fiber optics, which now account for about $60 million a year but are estimated to explode to $1.2 billion by 1990. Still, this is not putting copper out of business, and the Copper Development Institute says that by 1985 fiber optics will replace only 1 percent of the copper market.

But what is fiber optics? It is very high purity quartz doped with germanium and silica tetrachloride to develop high light refraction in the glass fiber. The system comes into action only if you add to it light emitters and detectors that are made of gallium, indium, and other sensor device metals. That market is a mere $15

"STRATEGICS": SOME HIGH-TECH STORIES

million now, but it's expected to grow to $100 million by 1985–86 and hit more than $300 million by 1990.

Why is fiber optics a sure bet? There will be a lot of copper in telecommunications for a very long time, but fiber optics has an advantage that just has to be used: It is immune to electronic interference. It may even survive the electromagnetic pulse (EMP) of a nuclear explosion that would knock out radio, computers, microwave, and electric power. You cannot tap or electronically intercept fiber optic transmissions, and that's important with all those Soviet trawlers snooping electronically all over the world.

Nuclear Weapons, Reactors, and Proliferation

Nuclear industry immediately evokes tales of hijacked uranium shipments, doomsday, and nuclear terrorism. The fact is we are in a nuclear era whether we like it or not, and whatever the provisions of international agreements nuclear weapons will be developed and tested and possibly even used. To think otherwise is just hiding your head in the sand. Nuclear power is already providing a significant proportion of electric energy in many countries, and despite protestations and setbacks that industry will continue to expand.

All this would not have been possible without the availability of numerous strategic metals that are critical to nuclear power. Most of the zirconium produced in the world ends up in fuel cladding materials. Cadmium, indium, molybdenum, and silver are used in reactor control rods production. Beryllium, columbium, rhenium, tantalum, tungsten, and vanadium are also vital to nuclear equipment manufacture and uranium processing. Germanium, thorium, indium, gold, and thallium are important in the production of radiation detection equipment. Iridium lines containers for radioactive substances.

Uranium is of course the prime nuclear fuel, but man-made plutonium and thorium are also nuclear fuel materials. Lithium is required for the thermonuclear power plant of the future. Several very little known heavy elements are also highly radioactive, including actinium, protactinium, neptunium, americium, curium, berkelium, and californium. But you won't be investing in those.

The question with strategic metals for this industry is tied to the question of proliferation. If stricter controls are imposed as a result of nuclear terrorism, black markets may develop, prices escalate, and government control of ownership may come into play. Think about it and don't get stuck.

Aircraft Are Strategic Metals Conglomerates

This is the world of superalloys where specific strategic metals such as cobalt are almost irreplaceable. In earth-bound vehicles and structures that collapse at first, the manufacturers can just slap some more metal onto it. In aircraft you do not get a second chance, so engineers are constantly figuring out how to make it go faster, carry more payload, and keep it from breaking up. A bigger engine used for more speed will require more fuel and a stronger structure—and then it turns out the engine is too small to lift the damn thing off the ground. Optimisation is the name of this game and strategic metals and superalloys are the ultimate solutions.

The jet engine, the heart of any modern aircraft, has developed into a truly remarkable conglomerate of superalloys. It takes ten years to design and test such an engine, and if you're suddenly denied cobalt in the process, this becomes very serious. The superalloys are mostly based on cobalt, which accounts for 22 percent of all elements used and is the most critical metal because it has strength at very high temperatures. What's more, 83 percent of all superalloys end up in jet engines and power gas turbines. Nickel, titanium, molybdenym, chromium, tungsten, columbium, and tantalum are the other metals of importance but their use ranges from 7 percent to 3 percent and less. Substitution of one metal for another must be watched for.

There is not much worry here about price escalation because the technical design value added in a jet engine is so overwhelming that doubling or tripling the prices of the materials only adds a miniscule percent to the total price. But designers are working around the clock to learn how to replace something like cobalt because supply disruption can not be tolerated.

Did you know that the Japanese have decided to establish an aerospace industry of their own to compete in world markets? They even want to build a shuttle of their own, more efficient than

"STRATEGICS": SOME HIGH-TECH STORIES

the Columbia, and export these to anyone with an urge to conquer space or experience some weightless fun. Having seen what the Japanese have done in electronics, you must take this decision very seriously. The implication, though, is clear. The Japanese will need increasingly more strategic metals and since they have absolutely no minerals in Japan they will have to get them from the world markets and increasingly compete with everybody else. Of course the Third World countries are getting together to see how to exploit the situation. They have never had such an opportunity before and it would be foolish to assume that they will not take advantage of these developments.

Last but not least are the private rocket and satellite builders and assorted nuclear weapons amateurs. In August 1981 the Percheron rocket built by a California firm fizzled out in a Texas cow pasture in an attempt to put a 3,300-pound satellite into orbit by a private group of Texas investors. Another, better known private venture is the West German OTRAG which is said to be backed by 1,400 investors who have already put up $69 million. Their operations are based in the congenial climate of Libya. There are many more such firms in operation and there is growing concern that their missiles could be used to threaten or deliver nuclear or chemical warheads.

Because such operations are literally dead without a supply of high quality strategic metals, chances are that governments may prohibit the sales of certain strategic and critical metals to such organizations. Such action may lead to the development of black markets for several strategic aerospace metals, as it has already led to surreptitious purchases of uranium by various countries. Any availability restriction will of course lead to shortages and price escalations of strategic metals. Ironic, but the spread of international terrorism is good news for strategic metals investors.

Then There Are All the Ferroalloys

Some of the strategic metals are never used in their pure state but form important alloys with other metals and are traded in that form. The most important of those are the ferroalloys that go into the making of various steels.

The strategic metals involved are chromium, silicon, manganese, molybdenum, titanium, and vanadium, and it is no accident that those metals are traded in such relatively large quantities. The iron and steel industry is the largest metals industry there is and is basic to any modern economy. While the steel industries of the world are in a state of depression due to economic downturns in the industrialized world, the Third World is busy developing its own steel industries and will soon consume increasing amounts of those ferroalloys as well.

Ferrochrome and ferromanganese may also present a different type of problem in the future. South Africa and Zimbabwe dominate the world in chromite and manganese production and reserves. There are indications that those countries are concentrating control over a very large part of global ferrochrome and ferroalloys production. Watch those areas for potential price-fixing action in the ferroalloys markets.

Increasing Demands for Pollution Controls

When the automotive emission control standards were set, catalytic converters made with platinum and palladium came into use to reduce exhaust hydrocarbons and carbon monoxide. By 1981 a move was on to make control of nitrogen oxides in auto exhausts mandatory as well. For this an additional catalyst is required in the form of rhodium. But when somebody figured out how much rhodium will be needed to comply it turned out there is not enough of it being produced in the world to do the job. To get more you would have to produce tons of platinum as well, flood the market, depress the prices and make a lot of people very angry. Quietly they delayed the restriction until 1985, but not before rhodium scored a fantastic run-up in price.

The environmental pollution controls will not go away, and work continues to improve the converter to use less rhodium or some other more efficient catalyst. If you can discover what that will be you've got it made. If not, acquire some rhodium before it escalates in price again by 1985.

Incidentally, automobile emission controls are primarily being enforced in the United States and Japan. Other countries are standing in aisles waiting to see what happens but there is the potential of a global demand as the fashion spreads. There is also

"STRATEGICS": SOME HIGH-TECH STORIES

the downside risk of a completely new catalyst metal being developed, but even then rhodium looks good because of the space war potential that is bound to come and clean up all the rhodium there is. It seems you can't lose on that one either way.

And Don't Forget the Chemicals

Chemical and petrochemical industries depend on availability of practically all the strategic metals, and those industries are also very large consumers of those metals. This fact is often forgotten because the metals are used in the form of compounds and salts, but these are just as critical to the production of chemicals as metals are to the manufacture of equipment.

The chemical industries are by far the largest consumers of antimony and bismuth, and the second largest or comparable end user of many other metals. This is especially true in the case of cadmium, cesium, cobalt, magnesium, and strontium. Other strategic metals such as manganese, molybdenum, palladium, platinum, rhodium, selenium, silicon, thallium, tin, titanium, tungsten, and vanadium are also consumed in significant quantities.

Rhenium, cobalt, and platinum metals also play a very important role as catalysts in oil-refining and petrochemical processes. Catalytic use of various strategic metals is still little understood and intensive research is under way. There may be significant breakthoughs in this area, causing investors to stampede into catalytic metals that also happen to be precious, inert, scarce, and expensive.

chapter 2
"The Gold of the 1980s"?

Well, the gold of the 1980s they ain't, but that does not mean that there are not some very exciting investment opportunities among strategic metals.

"Gold of the 1980s" is somewhat deceptive, and seems to have been introduced by the gold bugs of the 1970s who scrambled for a story to sell to the public after the gold market took a nose dive in 1980. It probably originated in London where the professional British minor metals traders began offering strategic metals as "an investment of the 1980s."

The gold bugs figured out that if you missed the gold rush of the 1970s you might be tempted to get in on the strategics bandwagon of the 1980s and incidentally keep them in business as well. If, on the other hand, you lost your shirt on gold, well, here they were ready to give you another chance with strategic metals. They would gladly exchange any gold you had and now hated so much for whatever strategic metal took your fancy. They really did not know very much about strategic metals but they figured correctly that you probably knew infinitely less.

Actually there are similarities and differences between gold and strategic metals. The similarities can be demonstrated by taking a dozen or so of the most active strategic metals like chromium, cobalt, columbium, indium, magnesium, molybdenum, rhodium, silicon, tantalum, and tungsten and showing that their prices during the 1970s skyrocketed pretty much like gold, keeping way ahead of inflation and any returns offered by other investments

"THE GOLD OF THE 1980s"?

such as bank deposits, stocks and bonds, or real estate. Of course, just like gold most strategic metals have fallen in price since then. So much for the similarities.

The differences boil down to six major ones all spelled the same way: liquidity, liquidity, liquidity, liquidity, liquidity, and liquidity. That's because with gold you can invest in six different ways. You have Kruggerrands and coins, bullion, futures, gold mining stocks and mutual funds, jewelry, and gold certificates. All gold investments are more or less liquid and if it came to a personal crunch your bank might even take them as collateral for a loan. How do you think they would treat you if you showed up with a bag of shrink-wrapped broken cathodes or flakes of a metal they never even heard of? That's the test of liquidity.

Every year the whole world produces close to 40 million troy ounces of gold, worth about $26 billion when (1980 average) gold is selling at $650 per ounce. In addition, if all the monetary gold reserves held by governments and central banks of the world are counted, an enormous sum of over $600 billion results.

Well, the annual production of all the thirty-odd strategic metals all over the world is estimated to be worth no more than about $18 billion. That's 30 percent less than gold. The markets for some strategic metals are so thin that they are measured in terms of a few tons and are worth but a few million dollars. The American stockpile is the only significant inventory of strategic metals, but only part of its $14 billion value is represented by strategic metals anyway.

The reason for this scarcity of strategic metals is not necessarily low occurrence in nature, as is the case with gold. The so-called crustal abundance estimates suggest that there are 100 parts per million by weight of chromium in this good earth, which is more than copper, nickel, or zinc, all of which are mined in large quantities. It is the economics of production and actual use that really determine the availability of those metals in the final analysis.

Many Are More Precious than Gold

If you define precious as being very fine, then platinum, iridium, and rhodium are indeed even finer than gold because these metals are very inert and cannot be corroded. If price is your yardstick, then those qualities are reflected in their price—those metals have traditionally been more expensive than gold.

Another way of looking at it is to see how scarce metals are in the crust of the earth relative to one another. See Figure 1. Here again rhodium and iridium as well as ruthenium and rhenium are several times scarcer than gold.

But the most interesting relationship between all metals shows up when you figure out all the prices for the same amount of each metal—in dollars per pound is very convenient—and then compare these to total production or consumption of each metal (see Figure 2 on page 23). What you get is a band of values showing that, whatever the metal, the more it gets produced and consumed, the cheaper it becomes. Only gold, platinum, and silver buck the trend of late presumably because of the "special monetary and jewelry" role they play.

Thus a frightening thought comes to mind in connection with this price-production relationship of metals. If new markets for strategic metals are developing (and more will emerge) the metals could become cheaper in the long run. Even so, this does not mean that there will not be many opportunities to cash in on price escalations before production catches up or substitution makes a metal worthless. That is the downside risk in this game. Does that mean you have to get rid of them while they're still precious? You bet your ingots. And fast.

Actually all serious minerals and metals economists will tell you that on the average over the years metals and minerals have either kept their value or have become slightly cheaper in real terms when their prices are adjusted for inflation. But after all that's what you're after. So you cannot complain. All you have to do is simply stay away from those metals that are likely "to become slightly cheaper" in real terms in the long run.

These arguments are based on averaging prices of all the metals including the basic metals, but many strategic metals appreciated in value significantly even in real terms, which is why they are so attractive. If you can pick those, you are "making" money. The problem is that strategic metals account for a very small percentage of the total metals market, and their performance gets lost in the averaging shuffle. Because they represent thin markets of vio-

Figure 1: **Abundance of Strategic Metals in Earth's Crust**

Metal	Parts per million by weight
Silicon	277,200.00
Magnesium	20,900.00
Titanium	4,400.00
Manganese	1,000.00
Strontium	300.00
Zirconium	220.00
Chromium	200.00
Vanadium	150.00
Zinc*	132.00
Nickel*	80.00
Copper*	70.00
Tungsten	69.00
Lithium	65.00
Tin	40.00
Yttrium	28.10
Columbium	24.00
Cobalt	23.00
Gallium	15.00
Molybdenum	15.00
Thorium	11.50
Cesium	7.00
Germanium	7.00
Beryllium	6.00
Arsenic	5.00
Hafnium	4.50
Uranium	4.00
Thallium	3.00
Ytterbium	2.66
Tantalum	2.10
Antimony	1.00
Mercury	.50
Bismuth	.20
Cadmium	.15
Indium	.10
Silver	.10
Selenium	.09
Palladium	.01
Gold	.005

*Base metals—included for comparison purposes.

Abundance of Strategic Metals in Earth's Crust
(continued)

Metal	Parts per million by weight
Osmium	.005
Platinum	.005
Ruthenium	.004
Iridium	.001
Rhenium	.001
Rhodium	.001

lent and frequent price fluctuations, however, they offer speculative opportunities.

Opportunities abound, but you are up against the liquidity question because there are no exchanges or established markets for most strategic metals. You will also have a hell of a time trying to outguess the professional metals traders. You will not be competing fairly unless you become one yourself.

A Tangible and Useful Asset

There is no question that metals, whether precious, strategic, or even basic, are a useful commodity. Why else would anyone go to all the trouble of producing them? Most minor metals were identified as elements during the nineteenth century; many have been nothing but a laboratory curiosity for decades. Now it seems at least thirty of the sixty-five metals that occur naturally have found a use in one or more industries.

Once a metal has come into use it also acquires a following of consumers, traders, and metallurgists whose livelihoods may even depend on its applications. Some of them are hard at work searching for new uses of their pet metal. For most metals there exists a specialized association or institute that is in fact lobbying for expanding the use of the metal. However, if the uses begin to dwindle those same organizations can become very annoyed and quickly turn into production control and price-fixing quasi-cartels. In a way there is someone out there looking out for each metal's interest.

Figure 2: **Relative Price-Supply Relationships of Strategic Metals**

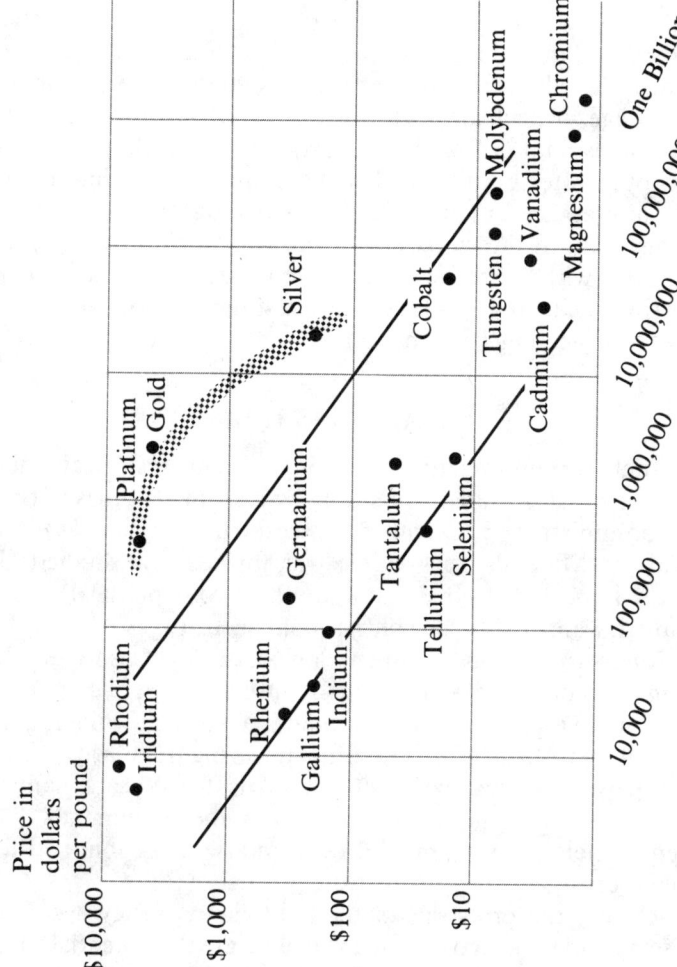

HOW TO INVEST IN STRATEGIC METALS

From an investor's point of view strategic metals represent an asset that will store value as long as there is a use for it. The advantages of such an asset lie in the fact that it is indeed tangible; its value cannot be depreciated by government decree, and it will not rot or often even burn. The disadvantages are that it does not bear interest, may require warehousing and insurance, which costs money, and in the worst case some smart scientist could always come up with a cheaper substitution that will make your metal worthless. Clearly, as with other investments, diversification is the key to protecting your metal assets.

Public Awareness Is Mounting

Much current impetus behind investment in strategic metals is being generated quite incidentally by certain attitudes of the Reagan administration. Even before President Reagan was elected, a Strategic Minerals Task Force was formed that studied United States import dependence on supplies from politically unstable countries and its impact on national security.

Congressmen, businessmen, lobbyists, and assorted self-proclaimed geopolitical experts made numerous public appearances pointing to a growing threat of potential strategic minerals supply disruptions. Articles have been appearing regularly in leading newspapers and magazines during the last two years, hammering home this theme and calling for new domestic minerals development policies, environmental restrictions relaxation, and foreign policy changes.

Some of the proposals of the politicians, if they ever come to pass, would in fact go some way to alleviate the potential shortages threat and strategic materials price escalations. But this would also be counterproductive from the investor's point of view. If you sank your savings in a few tons of cobalt and want to see it appreciate in value you must hope for upheavals in Zaire and prohibition on opening up public lands exploration. Otherwise no shortages will occur and you may lose your shirt, or at least not keep up with inflation.

Strategic metals brokers and various investment planners saw this opportunity to exploit the mounting public debate about strategic minerals policy issues to make some quick profits. They have further added to public awareness of the potential threats without bothering too much to explain the possible solutions and alternatives.

As a result, a market psychology is developing that continues to make strategic metals appear to be an important and potentially profitable investment opportunity for the 1980s. Since the politicians are certain to take their own sweet time before any effective legislation comes into play, most of the 1980s will probably continue to offer an excellent climate for strategic metals investment.

Inflation Is Driving a Search for New Investments

Continuing inflation assures the rise in cost of production and ultimately the price of commodities. Since many experts now believe that a high rate of inflation will continue for the foreseeable future, there is a constant search going on for tangible assets in the form of useful commodities that can last with relatively little attention and will increase in price, at least keeping up with inflation and hopefully doing even better. Strategic metals are just such a commodity.

The appeal of strategic metals as an inflation hedge stems from the fact that they have the potential for price appreciation not only as a result of increasing production costs, but because many strategic metals originate in politically unstable regions with significant potential for disruption of supplies due to political unrest, terrorism, transportation stoppages, and cartel-like production and price controls. Not only that, such disruptive activities, many of which are quite predictable, may combine to happen all at once.

All you have to do is to keep track of who is doing what and to whom in the major strategic metals supplier countries and you will soon find out that metal prices are sensitive to political developments. One British mutual fund, for example, is so convinced of major future upheavals in South Africa that it invests in shares of corporations that mine and produce all the metals that are threatened in that area. The managers of this fund specifically avoid South African producers concentrating on companies in Canada, Australia, and the United States. This fund also keeps a part of their funds invested in precious and strategic metals of the threatened areas.

HOW TO INVEST IN STRATEGIC METALS

Incredible Price Performance in Recent Years

Cobalt was an ideal strategic metal investment during the 1970s because it appreciated in price between 1973 and 1977 by 733 percent as a result of most of the factors described previously coming into play almost simultaneously. The reoccurrence of such a phenomenal increase is unlikely but certainly possible. Zaire and Zambia, where it all took place, are as shaky if not more so today. But let's not blame just the invading rebels from Angola for escalation of cobalt prices from less than $4 per pound to as much as $50 at the height of the cobalt shortage crisis in 1979.

The fact is that after the formation of OPEC oil embargo energy prices increased significantly, and this affected metals prices as well. Also, for several years during that period Zaire and Zambia had been reducing their cobalt production, and developments in Angola and Mozambique disrupted the fastest and most cost-effective transportation routes. The invasions of the rebels, whether Cuban-supported or Soviet-inspired, came at the end of this period of reduced production and were too short-lived to disrupt production very significantly at that stage. Nevertheless, these political events contributed tremendously to the scramble for cobalt that ensued, the emergence of a free cobalt market, and the rapid escalation in price.

The prices of many strategic metals have risen during the 1970s, reflecting a change that is beginning to take place in the traditional methods of Third World mining production and marketing. Long-term contracts at fixed prices between producers and consumers are rapidly becoming a thing of the past and governments are increasingly assuming control of their mining industries and metals marketing organizations.

As a result of all these forces, which are still in formative stages in many parts of the world, prices of many strategic metals have become unstable. This became particularly pronounced during the 1970s and is expected to continue during the rest of this century.

Most metals have shown significant price increases during the 1970s, although some have peaked in different years. Suffice it to say that at least fifteen strategic metals increased in price between the early 1970s and 1980 by factors ranging from 225 percent to as much as 2,000 percent, averaging about 800 percent to 1,000

"THE GOLD OF THE 1980s"?

percent for the period. This was more than enough to draw the attention of the investment community and thus the strategic metals investment industry was born. Today the investment industry is only looking for a means of increasing its liquidity—its basics are fairly sound.

Among the strategic metals that appreciated the most during the 1970–1980 decade were columbium, indium, tantalum, titanium, and tungsten. Their prices increased about tenfold during that period. The next best performers were germanium, molybdenum, rhenium, tin, and zirconium, appreciating about 50 times in value. The poorest of the lot were ferrochrome, manganese, magnesium, tellurium, and vanadium, increasing in price only between 2.5 to 4 times during the decade. This is still remarkable if you keep in mind that these metals are primarily consumed by the steel industry, which had been in serious decline throughout the world during that time.

chapter 3
Criticality: Availability

Criticality of a particular strategic metal varies according to who is concerned. Molybdenum, for example, is extremely critical to Western Europe and Japan because they must import most of it. It is *not* critical in the United States, which happens to be the largest producer of molybdenum in the world and accounts for 60 percent of global output of that metal. On a national basis import dependence on foreign sources is one measure of criticality. Within an industry the critical metals are those that are needed for manufacture of that industry's products and for which no substitutes exist. For a corporation only a few metals are critical, but competitive factors come into play, and cost and prices are critical.

For the investor all of those factors are significant because he is trying to single out a number of metals that are the most critical to the largest number of countries, industries, and manufacturers. This can be done by developing a criticality index for each metal. Such an index assigns a value to each factor from an investment point of view and rates all the metals relative to each other.

Some metals are critical because they are mined and produced in only a few countries of the world. This means that there are not many alternatives if one or more sources of supply are cut off. Industrial end-users of such metals will pay any price to get them in order to keep their programs going—particularly if military procurement is involved. Do not kid yourself, though. If the dis-

CRITICALITY: AVAILABILITY

ruption is prolonged and the price levels too high the end-users will develop a substitute material eventually.

Platinum metals are an excellent example of strategic metals whose sources are very few in number. South Africa and the Soviet Union produce about 95 percent of the global supply of all the platinum group metals. Canada, the United States, and Colombia make up the rest of the world's supply. There are also known deposits of significance in Zimbabwe.

But when it comes to those other platinum metals like rhodium, iridium, ruthenium, and osmium, the supply situation narrows even further. All these other metals are by-products of platinum refining, but they constitute only 1 to 2 percent of the total platinum output. Production of rhodium and iridium could be increased significantly only by flooding the world with platinum and palladium, which would both nosedive in price.

The Russians or the South Africans will not do anything that stupid to themselves as long as they control 95 percent of the world's supplies. The Russians may not talk to the South Africans for political reasons, but when it comes to sales of gold, platinum, chrome, and vanadium they like to involve themselves in what is called "collusive price leadership" of South Africa and "cooperate with world prices."

Gallium and germanium are two other strategic metals that originate from only three or four countries each. In the case of gallium, the major producers are aluminum and zinc processing plants in Switzerland and the United States. They can easily manipulate the price of gallium, but if it goes too high other alumina and aluminum and zinc producers will find it profitable to jump into the fray with their scrap material as well.

A similar number of countries produce germanium but present a somewhat different geopolitical setting. Germanium comes from Zaire, the Soviet Union, Namibia, and the United States. This shows the need to assess the sources relative to their political and ideological setting. An exploding demand, a revolution in Zaire, and a Soviet decision to expand their space effort may create quite a crunch on germanium. It will not last forever because there is a lot of germanium in coal and in old electronic scrap. If prices are right that is where the producers will find it.

Columbium is mined in six different countries, with Brazil by far the major supplier and automatic price leader for this metal. Rhenium is also produced in only six countries, but the United States and West Germany dominate this production so it is not unlike the gallium situation.

Other strategic metals that are produced in fewer than ten countries each include beryllium, cesium, indium, lithium, magnesium, manganese, scandium, selenium, strontium, tellurium, thorium, titanium, vanadium, and zirconium. The important thing to remember is that in most cases only three or four countries are significant producers, accounting for 70 percent or even more of global production. Thus the sources are actually few.

On the other hand, in a few instances sources may exist in many more than ten countries but the concentration of significance is in only a few. Cobalt and chromium are the best examples of such strategic metals because sources of these exist in seventeen and twenty-nine countries respectively but overwhelming concentrations of production and reserves in only a few.

Unavailable in Industrial Countries of the West

Another way of looking at criticality of strategic metals is to identify those that are not mined in the industrialized countries of the West or Japan, where the major markets are. You might as well start with the basic metals here because all the minor metals are more often than not their by-products. So it follows that if there is little or no mining production of basic metals many strategic metals must also come from imports.

Western Europe and Japan must import a very high percentage of their demand for bauxite to produce aluminum, copper, lead, zinc, and iron ore. They are also almost 100 percent dependent on imports of strategic metals such as cobalt, chromium, manganese, vanadium, and tin.

In the United States it is possible to identify all metals for which no significant mine production exists at present. This does not mean that there is not some production of the metal itself but it is mainly the result of processing of imported ores. The trend in the Third World is to establish domestic ore processing and sell finished metals at considerably higher prices, so this situation is changing. On the other hand, most minerals processing is a very energy-intensive process, so unless a country is blessed with domestic energy supplies this may not be so simple.

At present the United States has negligible or practically no mining of bauxite, cesium, chromium, cobalt, columbium, manganese, platinum metals, scandium, strontium, tantalum, and tin. But there are some deposits of many of those metals in the country. If prices of imports become high enough undoubtedly some of those deposits will be mined profitably, but it would still take years before such minerals would come to market. For practical purposes the metals mentioned above are not available from domestic mines and the situation in western Europe and Japan is very similar if not worse. The only industrialized country that has them all or practically all is the Soviet Union.

Imported from Unstable Areas in Large Quantities

Now that you know which strategic metals are critical and not available from domestic sources you might start wondering how secure their foreign sources of supply really are. It turns out that for much of the western world South Africa is the major supplier of most strategic metals and minerals. At the same time that part of the world is far from being politically stable or economically secure and in recent years has become the theater of East-West confrontations as well.

The countries of southern and central Africa are a veritable treasure trove of strategic minerals. They produce at least 25 percent or more of the global supply of antimony, cobalt, copper, chromium, germanium, gold, palladium, platinum, rhodium, ruthenium, manganese, and vanadium. Even when you raise the level to 50 percent you still find that this area supplies at least that much of chromium, cobalt, gold, germanium, platinum, rhodium, and ruthenium to the rest of the world.

Zaire, which controls at least 40 percent of global cobalt production as well as germanium output, is probably the most shaky country in the region. As a result those two metals, while very critical to many high technology and military applications, are seriously threatened by potential political upheavals in that country. Namibia, the third-largest germanium producer, is certainly not a stable alternative source either. And let's not forget that

Zaire also sits on top of the largest tantalum reserves in the world, although it is not a major producer of the metal at this time.

The Most Threatened Strategic Metals

The many strategic metals that originate in South Africa and whose only alternative source of comparative size is the Soviet Union are the metals that are the most threatened with supply disruptions or severe price escalations in the future (see Figures 3 and 4).

Smaller demands for some strategic metals can be met from various minor alternative sources; not all the importing countries meet all their demands for those metals by imports from South Africa. However, the largest demand is that of the United States and a major portion of that demand can only be met by southern African sources. Japan, with its ambition to become the leading economy of the twenty-first century, is a very serious competitor for those resources. West Germany and France, who have traditionally relied on British and American firms to supply them with strategic metals, are now also undertaking more intensified independent action to compete for those minerals.

The United States has to import 50 percent or more of its demand for at least thirty different strategic metals. Many of those are the same metals whose production is concentrated in South Africa and the Soviet Union. The strategic metals investor should be familiar with those metals from the start and keep watching developments in southern Africa that may affect their supplies. That is where the most action is likely to be in the future.

If you now look around at who controls 50 percent or more of the total global production of those strategic metals you will find that fourteen of the twenty are still under control of the Soviet Union, South Africa, and Zaire. This is not only impressive but also gives a very clear indication of which are the most politically vulnerable metals. The selection boils down to antimony, chromium, cobalt, germanium, gold, iridium, manganese, osmium, palladium, platinum, rhodium, ruthenium, uranium, and vanadium.

A further practical selection could now be made by eliminating gold as a monetary metal and uranium as a strictly controlled

Figure 3: **The Most Threatened Strategic Metals**

Strategic metals over 50% imported by the U.S.		Over 25% of global supply from southern Africa and Soviet Union	Over 50% of global supply from southern Africa and Soviet Union	
Aluminum	94%	Antimony	Antimony	48%
Antimony	53%	Arsenic	Chromium	85%
Beryllium	42%	Beryllium	Cobalt	75%
Bismuth	92%	Chromium	Germanium	75%
Cadmium	62%	Cobalt	Gold	90%
Cesium	100%	Germanium	Iridium	95%
Chromium	91%	Gold	Manganese	62%
Cobalt	93%	Iridium	Osmium	95%
Columbium	100%	Manganese	Palladium	95%
Gallium	70%	Osmium	Platinum	95%
Gold	56%	Palladium	Rhodium	95%
Iridium	100%	Platinum	Ruthenium	95%
Manganese	98%	Rhodium	Uranium	56%
Mercury	49%	Ruthenium	Vanadium	82%
Nickel	73%	Scandium		
Osmium	47%	Tantalum		
Palladium	87%	Titanium		
Platinum	80%	Tungsten		
Rhodium	85%	Uranium		
Ruthenium	81%	Vanadium		
Scandium	100%	Zirconium		
Strontium	100%			
Tantalum	97%			
Thorium	85%			
Tin	84%			
Titanium	90%			
Tungsten	54%			
Yttrium	60%			
Zirconium	67%			
Zinc	58%			

material. From the United States point of view one would also tend to eliminate germanium because the United States is a major producer. But on second thoughts western Europe is not, so if trouble comes to southern Africa germanium prices will move up

Figure 4: **Politically Vulnerable Strategic Metals**

(In percent production or capacity by major producing countries)

Antimony	20% South Africa 20% China 17% Bolivia 10% Soviet Union		Manganese	44% Soviet Union 20% South Africa 7% Australia 7% Brazil
Beryllium	39% United States 18% Soviet Union 18% Brazil		Mercury	45% Soviet Bloc 18% United States 16% Algeria
Cadmium	23% Soviet Bloc 14% Japan 9% United States		Palladium	66% Soviet Union 26% South Africa 7% Canada
Chromium	36% South Africa 27% Soviet Union 9% Albania 6% Zimbabwe		Platinum	61% South Africa 31% Soviet Union 7% Canada
Cobalt	50% Zaire 12% Soviet Bloc 12% Zambia		Rhodium	58% South Africa 34% Soviet Union 8% Canada
Columbium	71% Brazil 16% Canada 6% Soviet Union 3% Nigeria		Rhenium	45% United States 18% Chile 18% Germany 9% Soviet Union
Gallium	41% United States 26% Germany 10% France 5% Hungary		Tantalum	16% Thailand 15% Malaysia 13% Australia 11% Nigeria 10% Soviet Union
Germanium	25% Zaire 18% United States 10% Soviet Union 10% Namibia		Titanium	63% Soviet Union 23% United States 11% Japan 2% United Kingdom
Indium	22% Soviet Union 13% Japan 10% Canada		Vanadium	32% South Africa 26% Soviet Bloc 17% China
Iridium	61% Soviet Union 31% South Africa 8% Canada		Tungsten	19% China 17% Soviet Union 7% Bolivia

CRITICALITY: AVAILABILITY

because Europe will depend more heavily on the United States for its imports of that particular metal.

The platinum group metals are all in this selection. Osmium and ruthenium have very thin markets, but nevertheless their prices do not necessarily move in unison with other platinum metals so they may offer unusual if limited investment opportunities. Rhodium and iridium are becoming increasingly important in defense and high technology.

Thus of the original fourteen the favorites are clearly chromium, cobalt, iridium, manganese, rhodium, and vanadium. Platinum and palladium also look good and you can play their futures markets in New York exchanges. If you watch Soviet–South African developments to keep track of the other strategics you will have no trouble knowing when to get in or out of platinum and palladium futures.

Who Can Form Producers' Cartels

Cartels can only succeed in creating a temporary shortage by cutting down production. The sharp price peaks in individual strategic metals suggest that cartel-like price action is attempted in most metals every few years. Legitimate political or economic events are often just excuses to create the appearance of a disturbance and mask the manipulations by the producers.

Producers' meetings take place at various times but it is not always easy to keep track of them. It can be expected that with the growth of the "free markets" for strategic metals short-lived cartels will continue to develop, creating sharp price escalations sometimes in cooperation with metal traders. What the strategic metals investor should do is follow such developments in some of the most critical and most politically threatened metals because that is where incentives to try some price action will occur.

Cartels are basically commercial enterprises, but if governments control mining output, political objectives may also come into play. When a country depends heavily on exports of metals for its foreign exchange there are always incentives to run up the prices because it brings in additional revenues without the need for increased taxation at home—a popular and profitable course of action, with wealthy foreign capitalists having to foot the bill.

HOW TO INVEST IN STRATEGIC METALS

Formal cartel-like organizations exist among producers of bauxite (aluminum ores), copper, and tin because these are big-volume basic metals. For years gold and diamonds have been under the control of South African producers with Soviet industry following "price leadership" of the South Africans. Business is business, say the Soviet bureaucrats, even though they would not be seen even talking to such ideological heretics.

The most important cartel to watch as far as the strategic metals investment is concerned is the Intergovernmental Council of Copper Exporting Countries (CIPEC from its French name) located in Paris. It groups Chile, Peru, Zambia, and Zaire. In 1974 they started cutting back on production of copper up to 15 percent, having first nationalized or obtained controlling interest of copper mines in their respective countries. Since then Australia, Indonesia, New Guinea, Mauretania, and Yugoslavia have joined the group. They control almost 40 percent of copper output in the world and over 70 percent of copper export trade. Not bad, but not enough because the United States and Soviet Union are also very large copper producers.

The CIPEC cartel is important because many strategic metals are by-products of copper although not all copper deposits are equally rich in strategics. In general cobalt, gold, platinum, selenium, silver, tellurium, and thallium are major copper by-products. We all remember what happened to cobalt supplies and prices after the CIPEC-inspired copper production slowdown in Zaire.

The Cobalt Development Institute, formed recently to counteract cobalt substitution among consumers, is pointing to possible cartel price action in cobalt once again. If substitution continues, it would make sense for cobalt producers to get rid of stocks and reduce production and thus try to force price runup by the mid-1980s before project redesign will eliminate cobalt from critical applications once and for all.

The International Tin Council is one of the oldest cartel organizations manipulating the supplies and prices of tin. It groups producers and consumers and attempts to stabilize tin prices by use of "buffer stocks" and "floor prices" for tin. Malaysia, Thailand, Burma, and Bolivia are members. Watch out for more action when and if China joins this lot. Columbium and tantalum are by-products of tin in some deposits, but otherwise tin production does not influence other strategic metals output.

Cartel action among zinc producers would have more effect because cadmium, gallium, germanium, indium, and thallium are all major by-products of zinc production. The International Lead and Zinc Study Group with strong United Nations backing may lead toward some production controls. This would be extremely difficult, however, because lead and zinc are widely mined throughout the world and there are already thirty-one member countries in the group.

There is a good potential for a cartel in tungsten, and attempts are believed to have been under way for years. An International Association of Tungsten Producers exists, but China, the Soviet Union, and Bolivia are the major producers. However, a total of thirty countries produce some tungsten, so it is not the easiest thing to lock this one up.

It may be easier with antimony because South Africa, China, Bolivia, and the Soviet Union control almost 70 percent of world production. The problem is getting such diverse partners together, but the first antimony producers' meeting was organized in Bolivia in October 1981. Watch out for some price action on this one because they have already cut down on production.

International Mercury Producers Association (the abbreviation is ASSIMER, after the French name Association Internationale de Mercure) also exists but neither the United States nor the Soviet Union are formally members of the group, and these countries control 65 percent of global mercury output.

The uranium cartel came to light in 1976 when twenty-nine uranium-producing firms were accused of price fixing. It came about when Australia, Canada, South Africa, France, and England all reacted to a banning by the United States of uranium imports for domestic nuclear reactors. While this went on tidy profits could be made in uranium oxide, whose prices rose from $6 per pound to $40 in a couple of years. If Namibia falls there could be a tremendous run on uranium once again.

Titanium has also been the object of some price-fixing action in recent years. Several large users in the United States resorted to litigation against producers. Titanium price escalation also prompted new production capacity to come on stream but experts predict three- to four-year cycles in titanium supply. Demand will continue.

Chromium in the form of ferrochrome appears to be another candidate for price action in the future as a result of the consolidation of ferrochrome production in South Africa. Associated with this action may be an attempt to control most of the ferroalloys' production, particularly those based on manganese and vanadium because South Africa has a commanding position in the production of those metals.

Last but not least we have Brazil, which controls 71 percent of columbium production, and the United States, with 60 percent-plus control of molybdenum output in the world. The Soviet Union has similar domination of iridium, palladium, and titanium metal and in all these cases it is a case of price leadership of the largest producer.

Finally there is the New International Economic Order (NIEO) concept that emerged at the United Nations in 1974. Interesting how they got around to it as soon as the OPEC oil cartel began squeezing oil supplies. In a nutshell NIEO wants Third World producer countries to set up international commodity agreements to "stabilize" prices. This may mean "buffer stocks" under control of producing countries, but the NIEO wants the rich industrialized nations to provide the funds and technology to do it. Nice for the NIEO if they can get away with it.

Small Quantities, Thin Markets, and Corners

We mentioned previously that the value of all the strategic metals production throughout the world amounts to less than the value of gold alone produced in a typical year. Of course this value depends on the prices and changes all the time but at least it gives you a measure of the magnitude of strategic metals markets as a whole.

Of the thirty or so strategic metals that we are considering most of the time, ten account for about 93 percent of all the value produced and naturally account for most of the trade (see Figure 5). Those metals include manganese, silicon, platinum metals, molybdenum, cobalt, chromium, titanium, magnesium, tungsten, and antimony. It is clear that these include most of the ferroalloy

Figure 5: **Estimated Value of World Production of Strategic Metals (Estimated for 1980 at average prices)**

	Millions of U.S.$
Manganese	3,795
Silicon	3,000
Platinum Metals	2,890
Molybdenum	1,928
Cobalt	1,200
Chromium	1,000
Titanium	950
Magnesium	775
Tungsten	700
Antimony	300
Vanadium	280
Arsenic	180
Tantalum	125
Germanium	120
Columbium	120
Cadmium	85
Mercury	80
Rhodium	75
Zirconium	60
Iridium	50
Selenium	30
Beryllium	30
Indium	25
Rhenium	25
Bismuth	20
Tellurium	10
Gallium	10
Lithium	6
Strontium	3

Total value
17,772,000,000
($18 billion)

metals, which when taken by themselves would in fact account for almost 60 percent of the value of all strategic metals produced. That leaves about twenty strategic metals that account for somewhere between $1 billion to $1.5 billion in production value, meaning that many of their markets are very thin indeed. Many of those metals have an annual volume of production worth less than $100 million, but most of those in the very critical electronic metals appear to have a very bright future. Because demand in electronics may come and go quite rapidly, however, and most are by-products of zinc, copper, or nickel, they are also susceptible to rapid price fluctuations.

It is also clear that there are many organizations in the United States and elsewhere in the world that could readily muster the relatively small amounts of capital to literally corner the markets for some of those metals. It has been done before and it will be tried again.

What the investor must do is discover as soon as possible whether a rapid price escalation of one or more of those thinly traded strategic metals is the result of a genuine surge in demand or an attempt to corner the metal that will soon make it tumble precipitously in price—perhaps even overnight.

This of course is easier said than done, but there are ways of keeping your eyes open. Those who are professionally involved in some high technology industries that use such metals should not find this difficult. Other investors can always fall back on trade and technical sources of the industries that would be the major new customers for the metal in question. Some ideas about sources of information for this purpose can be gleaned from the last chapter of this book under the high technology and military publications sections. There is really little excuse except excessive greed for getting caught in one of those corners.

chapter 4
Criticality: Substitutability

Technological innovation is a constant process that on the one hand comes up with cheaper substitutes while on the other gives birth to new products and systems that can trigger off a sudden upsurge in demand for one or more of those metals. The science of substitution is a sophisticated and complex one and my purpose here is only to bring it to the attention of the serious investor. In order to keep track of developments in this area it is best to monitor specialized magazines such as *Materials Engineering* or *Metal Progress,* or attend some of the conferences and symposia on this subject. You will find details on where to make suitable contacts in Chapter 15.

The Irreplaceables

Every man has his price, goes the old saying. And so with metals. Every metal has one or more substitutes. Don't believe a metals broker who tells you that there are no substitutes for a particular strategic metal. Chances are he does not want you to know, and he's a real disaster if he does not know himself.

Actually there are specific uses of certain metals that are very critical because substitutes are much more expensive or less effective. Keep in mind that metal producers and consumers are not a secret international brotherhood jointly conspiring to unload a lot of scrap on the unsuspecting public, but rather that they are waging an endless substitution battle.

The two competing groups are trying to outwit each other in admittedly a common but quite separate effort to make a profit. The producers have a vested interest in spreading the myth that their metal is irreplaceable, and they sponsor institutes and programs to develop new applications. The consumers are always searching for better materials to make a more competitive mousetrap. If "composites" or "synterials" can do the job at lower cost they will drop the most strategic metal like a hot potato. This is called technological innovation.

The best an investor can do is to find out how many other metals exist that could substitute on an aggregate basis for each strategic metal. Of course this is only an initial step because each metal has many applications and substitute metals may not apply to all. If you go through that exercise, you will probably know more than your metals broker about just how vulnerable the metal he is trying to sell you can be to substitution.

There are about thirty-odd strategic metals listed in Figure 6 that are critical in varying degrees in specific applications. Most have one or more substitutes that can be used in many of their aggregate applications, though not in all. The number of substitutes available, nevertheless, provides some measure of the overall criticality of every metal and could be considered one of the factors in your criticality index.

A test that you can make about criticality of strategic metals is to check if the substitute is more critical than the metal it is replacing (see Figure 7). For example, chromium can be substituted in some uses by cobalt and manganese, but if those happen to be more critical at a particular time than chromium itself, such a substitution does not improve the vulnerability of the end user. In this way many theoretical substitution possibilities can be eliminated as impractical from the geopolitical point of view.

Where Substitution Is Inevitable

It seems almost certain that the use of cobalt in critical parts of the jet engine is headed for elimination. The major cobalt producers, by manipulation of cobalt supplies in the past, have forced jet engine manufactures to look for substitutes. Now the cobalt producers have formed the Cobalt Development Institute,

Figure 6: **Critical Uses and Substitutes**

Metal	Most critical or predominant application	Number of substitutes available in all uses
Antimony	Ammunition, semiconductors	6
Arsenic	Semiconductors	2
Beryllium	Hard copper alloys	4
Cadmium	Night-vision devices	5
Chromium	Armor and stainless steels	11
Cobalt	Superalloys, jet engines	4
Columbium	Rocket engines	2
Gallium	Semiconductors	4
Germanium	Electro-optics	4
Indium	Infrared sensors	1
Lithium	Thermonuclear power	0
Magnesium	Aluminum alloys	6
Manganese	High-strength steels	0
Molybdenum	Military vehicles	9
Osmium	Electrical contacts	4
Palladium	Catalysts	6
Platinum	Catalysts	6
Rhodium	Nitrogen oxides catalyst	0
Rhenium	Oil-refining catalysts	0
Ruthenium	Microelectronic circuits	7
Selenium	Xerography	6
Silicon	Semiconductors	0
Tantalum	Electrolytic capacitors	2
Thorium	Nuclear breeder reactor	0
Titanium	Aerospace structures	3
Tungsten	Machine tools	8
Uranium	Nuclear fuels and weapons	2
Vanadium	High-strength steel pipes	6
Zirconium	Nuclear fuel cladding	4

Figure 7: General Basic and Strategic Metals Substitutes

General Basic and Strategic Metals Substitutes (continued)

	Rhenium	Scandium	Selenium	Silicon	Silver	Tantalum	Tellurium	Thallium	Tin	Titanium	Tungsten	Vanadium	Yttrium	Zirconium
Aluminum				●	●				●	●		●		
Antimony									●					
Arsenic		●												
Beryllium														
Bismuth									●					
Cadmium									●					
Cesium														
Chromium									●					
Cobalt														
Columbium										●	●			
Copper					●				●					
Gallium			●											
Germanium			●											
Gold					●									
Hafnium	●													●
Indium														
Iron					●				●					
Lead			●				●	●	●					
Magnesium									●					
Manganese										●				
Mercury														
Molybdenum	●									●	●			●
Nickel						●								●
Platinum Metals	●					●	●	●				●		
Rare Earths	●	●											●	
Rhenium										●				
Scandium														
Selenium														
Silicon		●	●											
Silver														
Tantalum	●			●						●				
Tellurium			●											
Thallium														
Tin														
Titanium														●
Tungsten	●											●		
Vanadium	●													
Yttrium														
Zinc						●	●							
Zirconium										●				

Source: U.S. Bureau of Mines

whose purpose is to encourage the use of cobalt and to prevent substitutions.

Jet engine manufacturers are working feverishly to reduce cobalt use in jet engines by 25 percent by 1984. These cobalt substitution efforts are expected to continue even if cobalt price drops to $12 per pound or less. General Electric and Pratt & Whitney are replacing cobalt in some superalloys for existing jet turbine blades but in the long run jet engine redesign is expected to eliminate the use of cobalt wherever possible.

NASA, the U.S. Air Force, and major aerospace firms are also working jointly on cobalt replacement in new high-temperature alloys. In one program cobalt was eliminated from turbine blades by use of tantalum and so-called rapid solidification methods. In another program NASA managed to cut cobalt use by 50 percent in turbine disks by use of molybdenum and nickel alloys. A California firm is developing an iron-based alloy that will operate effectively at over 1400°C. and can replace cobalt. These efforts also consider new alloy manufacturing methods that reduce use of cobalt through redistribution of the metal within the critical parts by concentrating it only in the rim of a turbine disk where very high temperatures are encountered.

There is little question that a lot of research into new materials is now concentrated on substitutes for the chromium, cobalt, manganese, and platinum metals that are so threatened in southern Africa. Government and industrial laboratories are developing a whole range of synthetic or man-made materials that are touted as the building blocks of the future.

These new "synterials," as they are dubbed, include reinforced plastics, superconducting alloys, surface-modified materials, electrically active ceramics, high-temperature ceramics, and electronic semiconductors. Some will use various strategic metals but others will eliminate those that are threatened by potential shortages or supply cutoffs.

Development of these new materials would have taken place whether or not supplies of strategic metals were threatened. Synterials can be designed precisely to conform to product specification, while use of strategic metals demands that the product be designed around the metal's characteristics. As far as the investor is concerned these new materials are some years from massive use.

CRITICALITY: SUBSTITUTABILITY

You can also be sure that strategic metals producers are watching those developments closely and are bound to engineer a few more price runups before giving up the production of those strategics that may be totally replaced by synterials by the next century.

Keep Track of Ceramics in Gas Turbines

The critical jet engine redesign, besides reducing use of cobalt, will also include high-temperature ceramics in its components. This material is extremely attractive to designers of gas and diesel turbine components because it replaces chromium, cobalt, tungsten, and nickel with nothing but silicon, carbon, and nitrogen. Ceramics are silicon carbides and nitrides, and the raw materials used are sand, coal, and air, which are abundant everywhere.

Researchers at the Ceramic Research Division of the Army Materials and Mechanics Research Center claim ceramic components would be 40 percent less dense than metallic alloys and could operate at higher temperatures, which automatically means more efficient engines. In an age of escalating energy costs this is a very important consideration. Again, it will be some time before the present engines are redesigned, but make no mistake about the significance of these developments.

What Are Composites All About?

Composites are lightweight materials made from glass or plastics that are often considerably stronger than steel and more resistant to the elements than metals. Organic, ceramic, and metal-matrix composites are being developed and tested.

Aerospace composites include low-weight silicon carbide fibers that are embedded in titanium or aluminum matrix to form high-strength materials for the aircraft structures of tomorrow. Some composites may even create a new demand for some strategics. For example, a ceramic fiber superalloy developed at NASA contains tungsten, rhenium, hafnium, and carbon and is four times as strong as conventional superalloys. So who needs cobalt?

At present composites account for 3 percent of aircraft structure, but some engineers predict that during the 1990s 65 percent of the average jet transport may consist of composites. Composite aircraft parts even as critical as wings have already been built and tested. The aerospace industry was always in the forefront of new materials development and that is where you will find indications of which strategic metals will be becoming less critical as time progresses.

Electronic Synterials Are Also Coming

Electrically conductive ceramics made from metal oxides will be extremely important in the future. Some will be synthetic organic metals made from what is commonly known as plastics. When such materials are doped with atoms of impurities the plastics have properties of metals or semiconductors even though no metal exists in their composition. They are superior to metals because they are lighter and their electronic properties can be designed into them through chemical means over a very wide range of values.

Solar cells, fuel cells, gasification of coal, and superconductor materials are the areas to watch for new uses of electronic strategic metals and synterials. In semiconductors, gallium arsenide is considered seriously as an alternative to electronic grade silicon, which at one time displaced germanium from its dominant use in electronics. Microelectronics and infrared detectors is where the future action will be, so keep an eye on what designers are planning for those computers of tomorrow.

chapter 5
What about Scrap Recycling?

Recycling is certainly worth thinking about. As prices of strategic metals go up, at some point it becomes worthwhile to start recycling used equipment for its strategic metal content. Scrap in ordinary times may be just junked, but suddenly those dirty machine shavings can become more valuable than metal ores.

Some strategic metals, particularly of the platinum group, are so expensive and also so inert in their use as catalysts that they are normally recycled as much as possible. Others are so diffused in their use as compounds that no matter how high the prices climb recycling is not practical.

New and Old Scrap

Most metals are recyclable but whether or not it is done depends on how easy it is to collect and process both new and old scrap. It comes down to cost of energy versus price of metal and profit. Old scrap is that recycled from used equipment. Energy is expended in running the grinding and electrolytic refining process and in collecting and transporting the used equipment containing the metal. New scrap is the pieces of metal resulting from cutting down large pieces while machining parts, cutting out shapes, forging, milling, boring.

When cobalt was in short supply some started collecting those machining chips and sent them back for remelting, saving up to 20 percent of the materials necessary for turbine disks in jet engines. There is a lot of recycling possible in industrial manufacturing operations when it comes to a real crunch.

Which Metals Are Recyclable?

Theoretically any metal can be recovered after its use but some metals are so diffused that no one bothers. Only about half of the thirty-four strategic metals listed in Figure 8 are being recycled or recovered in any significant quantities.

Some, like arsenic, beryllium, and thallium, are quite toxic and recovery could be dangerous unless performed by the original refiners. Others such as bismuth or strontium are so predominantly used in chemical and pharmaceutical products that it is very hard to generate scrap with significant concentrations of those metals to make recycling worthwhile.

In steel and basic metals industries recycling is big business and trade in scrap is an industry of its own. About 30 percent of stainless steel, 25 percent of aluminum, 25 percent of copper, and 20 percent of nickel consumption in the United States can be met from scrap, and those metals constitute the bulk of the recycling business. Improvements in recycling technology and advances in city and industrial solid waste management may increase secondary recovery of many metals in the future.

Now that strategic metals are under threat, conservation of strategics by waste reduction and scrap reclamation is under study by NASA. Cobalt, chromium, columbium, and tantalum are considered most essential from this point of view. Development of a national information stockpile has been suggested to keep track of consumption of these metals in specific products in order to reduce waste and increase recovery.

The U.S. Bureau of Mines forecasts that demand for scrap containing chromium, cobalt, magnesium, mercury, rhodium, tantalum, titanium, and tungsten will increase between now and the end of the century. On the other hand, it is not certain that demand for scrap of all strategic metals will continue to grow. This is a tricky business dependent on metal suppliers and producer prices in the first place. Rapidly growing scrap collection and recovery activity during periods of increasing prices are also a good indication that additional supplies are coming into the market, and prices will soften soon afterward.

Figure 8: **Percent Recovery of Metals from Scrap**

Metal	Recovery
Antimony	66% mostly from batteries
Arsenic	None
Beryllium	New scrap in producer plants only
Bismuth	Small amounts only
Cadmium	Practical for Ni-Ca batteries
Cesium	None
Chromium	9% from stainless steel scrap
Cobalt	8%
Columbium	Insignificant
Gallium	25% of semiconductor use
Germanium	50% of new scrap. Optics potential
Gold	44% of consumption from old scrap
Indium	Small amounts
Lithium	None
Magnesium	13% from old scrap
Manganese	Not significant
Mercury	12% of consumption
Molybdenum	Small
Platinum Metals	30% total refined, 16% of sales
Rhenium	Small
Scandium	None
Selenium	25% from electronics and photocopier drums
Silicon	None
Silver	52% of consumption
Strontium	None
Tantalum	3% of new scrap
Tellurium	Insignificant
Thallium	Insignificant
Thorium	Not at present
Tin	14% of consumption
Titanium	Small
Tungsten	17% of consumption
Vanadium	Small
Zirconium	Insignificant

There's Platinum in Automobiles

Much discussion already centers on the recycling of platinum and palladium contained in catalytic converters of automobiles. These contain up to 0.05 troy ounces of platinum and palladium. It is estimated that at least 90 percent of that amount is recovera-

HOW TO INVEST IN STRATEGIC METALS

ble. By 1985 nearly 200,000 ounces of platinum may be available from converters for recovery that would approach $100 million in value at current platinum prices.

One firm, Refinement International of Rhode Island, is already developing a national collection network for recovering spent automobile catalytic converters from scrap yards and auto wreckers. The company also designed a silver reclamation unit that costs about $250 and can be used by small dental and medical offices. Refinement International is one of the publicly traded companies listed on the American Stock Exchange and was formerly known as Ag-Met Inc. Interestingly, the principal shareholder in this firm is the French Empain-Schneider Group of Paris.

It is needless to say that South African platinum producers are belittling the idea of platinum metals recovery from spent catalysts. They point out that recycling will encounter the problem of extracting "gunk" collected within the converters during their life. If the South Africans act that way to protect their production perhaps there is something in platinum recovery.

And Gold in Them Thar Computers . . .

Electronics is a large user of precious metals, and as this industry explodes the demand for semiconductor metals and precious metals will increase. However, electronics also generates increasing amounts of scrap containing all the electronic strategic metals. The problem with this type of scrap is the cost of collecting old electronic equipment at central locations where electronic scrap processing can take place.

This may create new security problems for large computer users and other electronic installations. To a knowledgeable criminal they represent valuable electronic scrap already collected at one location, and all that is necessary to retrieve the scrap is to open up those computer back panels and pull out the circuit boards one by one. The next step is to make mush of them in a simple meat grinder or a good blender and throw the stuff into a fish tank with an appropriate solution into which a couple of electrodes are inserted, then plug the whole schmear into an electrical outlet. While gold and other precious metals collect at the cathode all you have to do is keep track of the prices and you're in business.

WHAT ABOUT SCRAP RECYCLING?

Several electronics strategic metals that are presently not recycled to any significant degree may offer greater potential in the future as electronic equipment that uses them starts flowing into the scrap heaps of the country. Selenium recovery, already at 25 percent of consumption, is expected to increase even further as more and more old Xerox machines get ready for the scrap heap.

Gallium and germanium are already recycled in significant amounts. Germanium, which was used much more in electronics during the 1960s, is also contained in many transistor scrap heaps in private or government hands. Watch out for the effect of that pile of scrap on the market when germanium prices climb too high.

Indium, rhenium, tantalum, and tellurium are not recycled in significant quantities as yet. As for indium, it is an electronics has-been, so there are large inventories around. However, tantalum, rhenium, and tellurium could present recycling opportunities. If you are stuck with some unsalable tantalum scrap at present, cheer up. You may make out yet in a tantalum recovery business of your own.

A Mobile Scrap-Recovery Franchise of Your Own

Because precious and strategic metals are so diffused in electronics scrap throughout the country and the world it is uneconomical to collect small quantities of electronics equipment such as are found in private households. However, collectively these represent a large volume of strategic and precious metals.

Ideas are being promoted to design a vehicle that would in effect be a mobile refinery operating in neighborhoods collecting electronics scrap, grinding it up and refining it as it went along. This way the cost of collection, transportation, and processing could be reduced and significant quantities of those metals could be recovered. Such mobile strategic metals refineries would be franchised in exclusive territories for a fee, in return for which the franchisee would obtain the right to lease or buy the equipment and perform the operation. Watch out for such businesses when prices of strategic metals start going up and shortages set in.

chapter 6
Stockpiles of Strategic Metals

Actually, strategic materials being stockpiled include metals as well as minerals, castor oil, feathers, iodine, and even opium. If you are wondering about that last one, it is intended for the mass official doping of a population that suffers excessive doses of radiation after a nuclear attack and would otherwise have to die in pain. That's nice and considerate, but let's get back to strategic metals.

The National Defense Stockpile Inventory of the United States, which is the granddaddy of them all, contains ninety-three different materials, of which fifty-nine are metals and metallic ores (see Figure 9). The overall reason for the stockpile is to make sure that the United States could carry on a major war during the first three years even if foreign supplies are disrupted and military procurement is stepped up. What is in the stockpile gives us a good idea which metals are strategic and critical.

Of course that's only as far as the United States is concerned. Our valiant allies in Europe and elsewhere must fend for themselves as far as their industries are concerned. Japan, for instance, with practically no domestic resources of strategic metals, had done little in terms of stockpiling until 1976 when they formed two stockpiling associations for stabilizing imports of basic metal ores. However, in 1981 Japan authorized a National Strategic Stockpile, which includes molybdenum. Molybdenum is not in the American stockpile because the United States produces 60 percent of the world's molybdenum, but it is critical to Japan, West Germany, France, and the rest of Europe, who must depend on imports.

Figure 9: **National Defense Stockpile Goals and Inventories**

Metal	Weight unit	1980 goals	Current inventory
Aluminum	ST	7,150,000	3,444,064
Aluminum Oxide	ST	638,000	263,292
Antimony	ST	36,000	40,730
Bauxite, refractory	LCT	1,400,000	147,599
Beryllium	ST	1,220	1,061
Bismuth	Lb	2,200,000	2,081,298
Cadmium	Lb	11,700,000	632,729
Chrome Metal	ST	1,353,000	1,173,230
Chromite, refractory	SDT	850,000	391,414
Cobalt	Lb	85,400,000	46,002,393
Columbium	Lb	4,850,000	2,510,549
Copper	ST	1,000,000	29,048
Lead	ST	1,100,000	601,051
Manganese Dioxide	SDT	87,000	258,089
Manganese Metal	ST	1,500,000	1,974,247
Mercury	Fl	10,500	191,391
Nickel	ST	200,000	0
Iridium	TrOz	98,000	16,990
Palladium	TrOz	3,000,000	1,255,003
Platinum	TrOz	1,310,000	452,640
Rutile	SDT	106,000	39,186
Silver	TrOz	0	139,500,000
Tantalum	Lb	7,160,000	2,392,072
Thorium Nitrate	Lb	600,000	7,146,327
Tin	LT	42,000	200,477
Titanium Sponge	ST	195,000	32,331
Tungsten	Lb	50,666,000	82,515,773
Vanadium	ST	8,700	541
Zinc	ST	1,425,000	375,946

Key to weight unit abbreviations: Fl = flasks; Lb = pounds; LCT = long calcined tons; LT = long tons; SDT = short dry tons; ST = short tons

Source: Federal Emergency Management Agency

HOW TO INVEST IN STRATEGIC METALS

Depending on who you are your motives for stockpiling one or more strategic metals will vary. One country's strategic metal may be another's surplus scrap. Governments of France, West Germany, the United Kingdom, Italy, Spain, South Korea, and Sweden have studied, financed, approved, or otherwise toyed with stockpiling ideas. In the final analysis the question revolves around who is going to pay for it. In any case the stockpiles, existing and proposed, are peanuts in comparison with those in the United States, which, incidentally, cause a lot of sleepless nights to some of the more nervous metals traders in the world.

This is because metals traders also maintain stocks of their own in order to meet market demand, but they are not too keen to tie up a great deal of capital in such stocks. Similarly, metal end-users protect themselves against raw materials shortages by keeping inventories in their plants. Neither wants to be caught with his pants down if a national stockpile, or a Soviet state monopoly for that matter, suddenly starts selling in large quantities.

The producing countries out there in the deserts and jungles where there is no consumption of these strategic metals have yet another reason for stockpiling. If they do not keep their mines operating they may have a revolution on their hands. If they export too much metal to the world, prices will collapse and their political enemies will grab the opportunity to accuse them of selling out to the capitalist exploiters. So they get together to form international cartel-like producer groups and develop "buffer stocks," inspiring naive young western journalists to write about their latest "price stabilization" schemes for the good of mankind.

As for the Soviet Union, they are sitting pretty. By accident of nature they have everything within their own borders, so they can stockpile by not digging it up if they choose to do so. They can swap some obsolete MIGs for cobalt for their own consumption and when shortages develop they can increase their own production and get some hard currency in the western markets as prices escalate. All they need is a "working stockpile" to best manipulate the markets and the secrecy laws to keep us all confused as to their intentions. They have been very good at it.

Last but not least as far as the reader is concerned are the investors with their strategic metals portfolios, mutual funds and trusts, or even a few troy ounces of rhodium in a safe trying to beat inflation and make a killing in the process. It can be done. But they must understand that they are but a minor element in an international geopolitical arena in which governments, multinational corporations, and global finance are the major players. Investors must make an honest effort to find out the rules of this game and learn how to spot where the action is going to be in advance. The investor must know what he is doing, or he will end up with a garage of tantalum scrap that the city will charge him to haul away.

chapter 7
Who Trades in Strategic Metals?

The private strategic metals investor and the average American strategic metals broker are in most cases both newcomers to the metals investment game. As such they are likely to be treated as the new kid on the block by the metals producing and trading professionals. Some outside investors with significant capital to invest will be tolerated by the industry primarily out of respect for the risk they are taking. But the professional metals trader will always look askance at the small investor with only a few thousand dollars to spare and his metals broker, whose small and frequent purchases are only marginal and bothersome business at best.

For those reasons investors or brokers who feel that strategic metals is their bag should learn all they can about the metals and minerals industry structure all the way from the mining operations through processing, trading, and consumption of metal. An educated strategic metals investor should at least be able to decide when he's had enough before he loses his shirt. A strategic metals broker, on the other hand, once he gets the hang of it all and still likes the game, will probably become a metals trader sooner or later anyway.

Where Do Investors Fit in the Metals Industry?

The private investor, which in all probability means the reader of this book, is part of but a very minor loop in the metals industry, as shown in Figure 10. He is at least three or four levels removed from the mainstream of metals trade in all its forms and he is insignificant in terms of trading volume. This is particularly true of the investor interested only in strategic metals, because these account for only a few percent of the overall minerals and metals trade.

Just how small that trade really is relative to the total minerals and metals trade is perhaps best illustrated by the relative investment levels in new mining projects. Out of a total of $100 billion earmarked for the development of about five hundred new projects during the 1979–1984 period throughout the world, strategic and minor metals, which are other than aluminum, copper, lead, zinc, nickel, gold, iron ore, and uranium, received a mere 3.6 percent of all the funding.

An ordinary small investor new to this business deals primarily with a strategic metals, commodities, or investment broker when he decides to invest in one or more strategic metals. He may also deal with a financial planner or accountant who in turn must fall back on a metals broker unless he knows better. The metals broker acts on behalf of the investor and buys strategic metals or shares of strategic metals funds, trusts, and limited partnerships if he is a licensed securities broker as well. If the investor prefers to buy actual metals rather than shares in a fund he must take delivery of the metal purchased and arrange for its warehousing, insurance, sampling, assaying, and accounting. Here the metals broker comes in handy because he should be familiar with all these matters.

If the investor chooses participation in one of the registered strategic metals mutual funds as a shareholder he is not bothered with all the associated problems of metal ownership. The fund manager who buys and sells strategic and other metals for the fund takes care of these matters as part of the effort of running his fund.

The strategic metals broker or fund manager relies primarily on the industry metals traders for the supply and purchase of strategic metals. If the broker or the fund manager is buying fairly large quantities of metals comparable to commercial transactions he may also go directly to the producers, but he is unlikely to obtain metals at prices better than those offered by the metal traders unless there is a glut in question on the market. Both strategic

Figure 10: **Structure of the Metal Trading Industry**

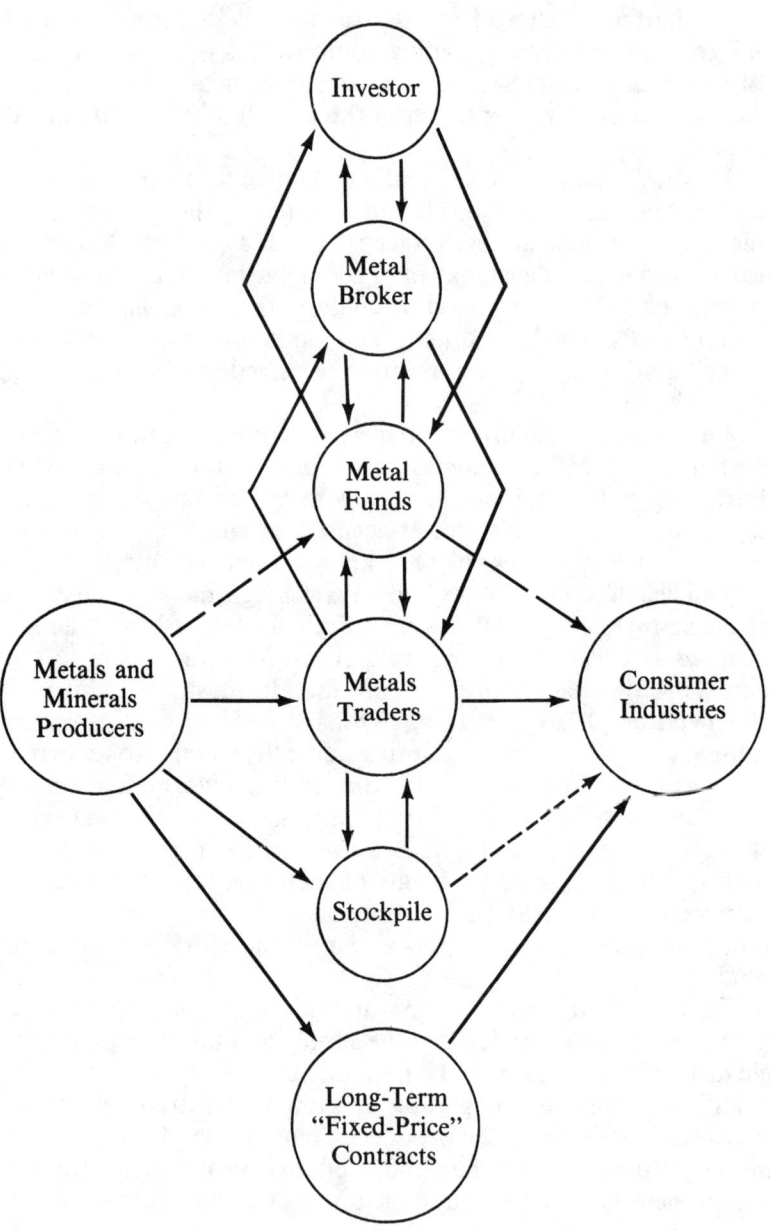

WHO TRADES IN STRATEGIC METALS?

metals brokers and fund managers may also try to sell their metal holdings directly to industrial end-users, but it is more likely that they will deal primarily with the metals traders, who are familiar with the end-user markets and will not take kindly to increased competition.

As far as an individual investor is concerned, all this would make very little difference to him if strategic and minor metals were traded at an established exchange with daily price quotations and the automatic market liquidity that such institutions offer. Alas, this is not the case—strategic metals are not traded on any exchange and all transactions are individually negotiated with metal traders. And there does not appear to be any prospect of an exchange for strategic metals coming into being because the overall trade is simply too small.

Strategic metals brokers only offer to sell metal on a best efforts basis—acting in such a case as if you (who purchased from him) were just another metals trader with metal for sale. If you are in a hurry to liquidate your metal holdings, the broker may offer you a price that will be only a fraction of what you paid, but he is not obligated to do so because he may not be able to sell the metal for some time.

As a result an investor buying strategic metals is entering what is basically an illiquid market comparable to the purchase and sale of real estate rather than securities. He can avoid that by specifically sticking to shares of strategic metals funds or commodity pools, which are either traded on a stock exchange or are redeemable by the fund itself under predetermined conditions.

Because of all these factors a private investor who buys strategic metals directly is really acting as a very small metals trader building up stocks for his own account in expectation of future profits. But since an investor is not a member of the metal trading community he is operating at a comparable disadvantage, and unless he is prepared to spend a lot of time and money on research he may have a hell of a time knowing when to sell his metals, aside from the fact that he would also have to find a buyer for his holdings.

The Role of the Metals Broker

The metals broker who buys strategic metals on behalf of an investor is basically just a salesman and middleman selling strategic metals for cash. He buys strategic metals from the metal traders who happen to trade in the specific metal you desire and who are willing to sell small amounts of metal through your broker. Many large international metal traders cannot be bothered with the minimum-size orders that a strategic metals broker may try to execute on your behalf and they will simply refuse to be involved in such business.

When strategic metals were first offered as an investment to the public in the United States during early 1981 most strategic metals brokers were previous salesmen or brokers of commodities such as gold and precious metals. They turned to strategic metals after gold and commodity markets took a nosedive during 1980. Strategic metals, dubbed by them "the gold of the 1980s," was a convenient and timely idea offering a certain amount of continuity and keeping them in a business that was otherwise severely eroding.

Those strategic metals brokers knew practically nothing about the metal trade outside of gold and precious metals when they started. It is interesting to note that they mostly drew their inspiration from a British firm that began promoting the sale of strategic metals for investment purposes in 1980. However, Strategic Metals Corporation of London, in contrast to most American self-styled strategic metals brokers, includes seasoned professional metals traders as principals. They developed a service for the purchase and storage of strategic metals on behalf of institutional and industrial customers.

Strategic Metals Corporation was an instant hit with the American brokers because it, as well as other British metal trading firms, was willing to accept and execute the small orders of the metals brokers. This firm also knew all the associated procedures and provided all the necessary warehousing, insurance, inspection, assaying, and documentation services.

The metals broker orders the metal from a metal trader either in London or in the United States on the investor's behalf. The metal trading firm then delivers the metal ordered by transferring a warehouse receipt for a particular lot of metal to the name of the new owner after receiving and clearing the payment.

A strategic metals broker must pay the asking price for the metal plus a commission and other fees, depending on his agreement with the metal trading firm. He does not execute an order

WHO TRADES IN STRATEGIC METALS?

in a market or an exchange like a stockbroker but negotiates each individual metal purchase with one or more metal traders supposedly in search of the best price.

Because these are cash transactions, once you decide to buy some metals you will be asked to send your metals broker the full amount of your purchase price estimated at the latest known price for the basic trading unit of the metal you are purchasing. The metals broker may charge you an initial account opening fee and buy and sell commission fees payable in advance. With the storage and other charges, up to 20 percent of the total purchase value may go toward meeting all those expenses in a year.

Since these are not liquid and instantaneous markets, the broker also may use received cash as part of a "float" account that gathers additional interest for him in short-term certificates. The opportunities are very tempting to play various games with customers' funds, particularly since this is not a regulated market and investors in many cases sign an understanding that it may take weeks or even months before they receive the final documents that establish their ownership of the metal they have purchased. Here, like in any other sales transaction, the investor should be extremely careful of who the broker is and what his track record has been in the past.

What is stopping the investor from doing business directly with the established and reliable metals trader? Nothing. All he has to do is find out who they are and which among them are willing to sell the metal in question. All the other warehousing and insurance arrangements can of course be equally well provided by the metals trader for basically the same fees, since he constantly does it for his industrial clients anyway.

If you choose to do it yourself, you do escape your broker's fees and commissions, but finding a metals trader that will do business with you may turn out to be a chore. Nevertheless, the choice is yours, and if you are spending in the hundreds of thousands of dollars on this game you will save a bundle by developing your own sources and in fact you will probably feel you are just a little more liquid in this illiquid market. Do not be deterred by the apparent difficulties of getting your own thing going. After all your broker started out just as ignorant probably only a few months ago, and now he is charging you commissions for basically knowing who the metal traders are.

HOW TO INVEST IN STRATEGIC METALS

Who Are the Metal Traders?

The metal traders are the professionals who make up the free market in metals. They trade in all the metals: mainly iron and steel, copper, aluminum, lead, zinc, nickel, and gold and precious metals, but they also deal in strategic metals as well. Many specialize in a group of metals such as ferroalloys, which in fact includes many strategic metals. Some but not all metal traders trade in strategic and minor metals. Only rarely does a metals trader handle all the strategic metals at all times.

Most metal traders are in business to supply established industrial consumers with raw materials for their manufacturing operations. Because the bulk of industrial metals consumption involves iron and steel and basic nonferrous metals such as aluminum, copper, lead, zinc, and nickel, that is what the metal traders handle the most. There are many metal traders who specialize in nonferrous metals only, but that means more often than not that they are mainly aluminum and copper merchants. They provide those metals to customers in all commercially desirable forms and are active in metals exchanges where the futures of these metals are being traded.

Metal traders are the professionals who know the most about the metal markets. They have to in order to survive because their major competitors are the metal producers themselves, who control the bulk of global metals trade through long-term contracts between themselves and major consumers. At least that is what the global metals trade was all about until the changes in political and trade patterns of the last twenty years brought more prominence and influence to the metal trader in global metals trade.

The metal trader was the original "investor" in metals, risking his capital on the expectation that metal consumers may develop a sudden upsurge of demand for one or more metals not predicted by the producers, who for whatever reason could not fill such orders. As such, metal traders were often regarded as parasites, but their speculative function is vital to the smooth operation of international metals trade.

Over the years the growth of free markets in metals outside the long-term "fixed" price producer-to-consumer trade has been spectacular. Inflationary pressures, political uncertainty, nationalization, and rapid shifts in some raw material markets due to technological change have taken the luster off the "fixed" contract. The free market is looked upon as the metals trading system of the future.

As a result the metal trader has come to new prominence in international trade circles, and some of the leading metals merchants are no longer engaged in only trading activity. They undertake the financing of new mines, provide technology for development, conduct metal market research, and all the remaining services required in processing, transportation, warehousing, and distribution of metals throughout the world.

Metals traders come in all sizes and shades. Some, like Phibro, are very large international organizations with metals trading subsidiary firms in major metals producing and consuming countries. Such firms are members of various exchanges where metals are traded such as London Metals Exchange (LME), New York Commodity Exchange (COMEX), New York Mercantile Exchange, Chicago Board of Trade, Hong Kong Gold and Silver Exchange, and other professional trade organizations.

Other metals trading firms, such as ACLI, are subsidiaries of investment firms or are partially owned by large international mining organizations. These firms are extremely powerful in metals trade and are very knowledgeable in the marketplace because they have the inside track of both the producer and the free market side of each story for most metals. This is what the strategic metals investors and brokers are up against when they are trying to make a killing in the metals trade.

Many metal trading firms represent specific metal producers either throughout the world or in selected markets, while other traders are relatively independent firms handling local distribution of metals and scrap materials. During the 1970s a trend began for American investment banking firms to show an interest in metals trade. Drexel, Burmham, Lambert of New York bought a British metals trading firm that gave them membership in the London Metals Exchange. Bache Halsey Stuart Metals, a subsidiary of the well-known investment firm recently acquired by Prudential Insurance Company, is another established metals trading firm that is also a member of LME. Other investment firms include Conti Commodities, the largest American commodities trading firm, which also trades basic and precious metals futures on most exchanges.

There are at least 1,200 nonferrous metal trading firms around the world. They are listed in the first directory ever compiled of such organizations, which was published for the first time in 1980. You can find more details about this publication in the last chapter of this book. The important thing to keep in mind is that potential profits in strategic metals is not a new development uncovered by your metals broker who may need your commissions. The metals traders have been at it for years if not centuries. If you want to keep even or hope to stay ahead in this game the metals trader is the guy to watch, regardless of what your broker says.

The Big Mine Producers and Traders

These are the companies primarily headquartered in the industrialized countries of the West that have traditionally controlled the markets in most minerals and metals traded in the world. What they do not know about the metals trade and price trends just isn't worth knowing.

The mining, processing, and manufacture of minerals and metals is the second largest industry in the world after agriculture in terms of people it employs and the earnings it generates. The capital requirements for the development of a typical mine are very large, ranging in the hundreds of millions of dollars, and the lead times from exploration to metal production may take up to ten years.

Only the largest corporations and governments with significant financial backing can afford to engage in large-scale mining. This explains the existence of the relatively few powerful mining organizations that control the bulk of this business and trade. Many of those corporations are veritable conglomerates of mining, smelting, refining, fabricating, and even final product manufacturing firms, integrated vertically and controlling the flow of metals all the way to the final customer. Some are even subsidiaries of large oil and energy resources companies, which is also important if you keep in mind that mining and metal processing is a very energy-intensive industry.

These major mining and metal corporations produce and trade

the lion's share of metals and minerals in the world. They are in a position to impose and maintain a producer price for their metals based on the long-term "fixed" price contracts that they sign with their major industrial customers.

These producer prices are generally observed by all competing mining firms and are often favored by the major consumers because a producer price assures a measure of price stability in the marketplace. It is important to the customer to be able to plan his production with some idea of what the costs of raw materials are going to be during the lifetime of a product. By the same token the producers are assured of a market for their output, which they have planned relative to costs of production that are likely to exist during the time when the producer price is in effect.

As a result, the big mining corporations exercise a very important influence on the trade and prices of all the metals. Because they are also the producers of most metals they obviously have considerable influence on the supplies and prices of metals that are handled by the metals traders in the free market. As previously mentioned, some of the largest metals trading firms are subsidiaries or agents of the producers anyway.

The emergence of the centralized communist mining monopolies and newly independent countries in Africa that are also significant minerals and metals producers is changing the traditional patterns of metals trade. Nationalization of mines and marketing organizations, previously controlled by the large mining conglomerates, also resulted in the development of new sources of metals and minerals available directly to the metals traders in the free market.

By far the greatest changes took place during the 1970s, due to global inflationary pressures that forced many producers to adjust their long-term prices more often and in some cases to abandon the producer price system altogether. This trend continues and is expected to be a major influence on the pricing and trade of metals in the future.

The State Quasi-Cartels

In many of the new independent countries of Africa and Latin America the mining industry is now controlled by the governments, either through ownership or mining legislation of the country. Since the emergence of the OPEC oil cartel many developing countries that are important suppliers of minerals and metals to the industrialized West have also considered the application of cartel principles to control the production and pricing of their non-oil minerals.

Such action requires intergovernmental cooperation, often between politically diverse governments, and is not easy to implement. But it also requires centralized control of the metals mining and marketing organizations in the countries concerned, and the governments of many developing countries have been moving in that direction relentlessly. In the process they had to nationalize the previous corporate owners and enter into new agreements with them for continuing operation of the mines and marketing of the metals. Clearly if agreements could not be reached the free market traders were ready and waiting to take up the slack. This situation had a profound effect on the changes occurring in the metals markets.

Today several developing countries have established one or more government-controlled mineral and metal producing or trading organizations that have virtual monopoly over all the metal products in their country. SOZACOM of Zaire, which is the leading supplier of cobalt in the world, and MEMACO of Zambia are good examples of such state-controlled metals trading organizations.

Those companies, which operate as national metals trading firms, set the prices of the metals produced in their country. If they command a significant share of world production they automatically become the price leaders for the metal. While they do take into account market demand in consuming countries, at the same time the governments of those countries assist their metals trading firms by controlling production and financing stockpiles of the metals if necessary. These are the "buffer stocks" that some of the cartel-like country groupings would like to set up on an international basis in critical metals. The stumbling block is the reluctance of western industrial countries to finance such stockpiles of metals under the control of international bodies. The producing countries themselves are not in a position to finance such operations as yet. It is important to keep in mind that as these countries improve their economies and reserves position they will sooner or later be able to set up such buffer stocks on their own and manipulate the supply of various strategic metals according to their political and economic requirements without too much concern for market forces.

There is also the possibility that wealthy Arab OPEC states may wish to provide the funds necessary to develop such stockpiles. The Arab-African aid programs have been developing quite rapidly. In most cases they have been directed against the South African policies, and it can be expected that this activity will accelerate in the future.

The State Monopolies

These organizations are unique to the communist countries, because of their centrally controlled economies. In general a ministry is responsible for all mining and metal processing and production proceeds according to predetermined five-year plans. In the initial years communist countries produced only enough metals for their own consumption, but with the development of their economies they began offering surplus metals production to foreign markets. Capitalist countries are the preferred customers because this provides communist countries with badly needed hard currency that can be used for the purchase of high technology goods and equipment not available within their own countries.

The marketing of strategic metals of communist countries is handled by specialized foreign trade organizations that are under the control of the Ministry of Foreign Trade. In the case of Albania, Angola, Bulgaria, Cuba, East Germany, Mongolia, and Vietnam, a single metals trading organization controls all the trade in metals. In the case of Czechoslovakia, Hungary, North Korea, Poland, Romania, the Soviet Union, and Yugoslavia, two or more metals trading organizations exist that are responsible more often than not for specific groups of metals. In all cases the central monopoly remains in the hands of the Ministry of Foreign Trade.

The state monopolies are an increasingly important factor in the global trade of strategic metals, and their actions and behavior must be closely watched by the strategic metals investor who wants to understand the developments in the market when certain strategic metals such as chromium, platinum, titanium, or beryllium are concerned.

The Soviet Union is the most important factor because of its sheer size and dominant position in the production of chromium, ferrochrome, cobalt, titanium, beryllium, platinum, rhodium, iridium, and a significant production of many other metals such as gold.

China is the second most important potential supplier of many strategic metals other than antimony, tin, and tungsten, which it is the dominant producer of. Recently China began offering a large array of strategic metals for sale including indium, germanium, and other electronic and aerospace strategic metals.

Of the remaining communist countries Albania is the third largest producer of chromite and its immediate recognition of the new Zimbabwe government in 1980, which controls some of the largest chromite resources in the world, gives much food for thought. Yugoslavia is a producer of several strategic metals in relatively small quantities. Cuba is a factor in cobalt supplies within the communist bloc. Angola is a potential future supplier of many strategic metals that are also available in geologically similar Namibia, Zambia, and Zimbabwe.

The communist state monopolies are particularly important because their actions are unpredictable and their intentions veiled behind much official secrecy and regulation. Sudden withdrawals of platinum and titanium from world markets by the Soviet Union in recent years illustrate eloquently the power and influence that those state monopolies can command at a moment's notice. You will do well to keep the Russians always in sight and keep track of what the Chinese are offering for sale.

chapter 8
Where to Find Strategic Metals Prices

One of the biggest problems in strategic metals investment is the lack of daily price quotations in the major public media. Prices of precious metals such as gold, silver, platinum, and palladium are quoted daily in major and even minor newspapers, on radio and on television. The prices of basic metals such as copper, nickel, lead, zinc, and tin are also available daily in major newspapers. But you will look in vain in any of those media for news on how your strategics are doing.

This chapter is designed to inform the strategic metals investor that there is no need to despair. There are actually even daily strategic metals price quotations available, but you have to know where to find them. It is paramount that as an investor you establish a source of strategic metals price information that is independent of your broker.

Don't Try to Call Your Investment Broker; He Has Never Heard of Yttrium

If you have tried, you know what I mean. When he asks you what is yttrium, or ruthenium for that matter, you know he does not know what you are talking about. Why should he? These are neither the names of companies whose stocks are traded on one of the exchanges, nor of commodities in the futures markets.

It cannot be emphasized too often that strategic metals are not traded on any exchange. Anywhere. Period. Not even over the counter, where a lot of the new stock issues make their debut. Over-the-counter markets operate according to public auction principles as do commodity futures exchanges. What this means is that somewhere there are one or more specialists who "make a market" in particular stocks or commodities. After a day of making such a market there is a record of latest prices bid and asked, the price changes during the day, and the amount of shares or contracts changing hands. No such specialists prepared to buy or sell at any time exist in the strategic metals field. Consequently, there are no consistent records and no central sources for price information.

In fact, the demand for some strategic metals is of such a nature that trades are few and far between. Sometimes weeks or even months may elapse before an end-user comes in with an order for a few tons of selenium. One or more of the metal trading firms will fill that order, record the price and quantity, and file away the data in their sales reports. It may never see the light of day again.

The reasons for this lack of a strategic metals exchange have been discussed at length already. Suffice it to repeat here that despite the criticality of many strategic metals in various military and civilian applications, the quantities involved are relatively small. Their respective markets in comparison with oil, iron and steel, basic metals, and gold are also insignificant. As a result even the global trade in strategic metals does not justify a central exchange, and there are no prospects on the horizon that such an exchange will come into being in the foreseeable future.

On the other hand, the metals traders and producers as well as consumers do have a need to keep track of metals prices to plan their production and purchasing strategy. For this reason a number of services collect and disseminate price information about the latest trades in most strategic metals. These price quotations reflect average prices computed from several quotations of metals traders who have recently sold a particular metal in question. But keep in mind that these are all individually negotiated transactions and prices vary depending on quantities purchased, form of metal, its purity, time of delivery, and other factors. Prices quoted do not necessarily mean that there is anyone anywhere willing to buy any quantity of the metal at or near the average reported prices. Figure 11 shows where to find strategic metals prices.

Figure 11: **Where to Find Strategic Metals Prices**

	American Metals Market	Chemical Marketing Reporter	Engineering/Mining Journal	Industrial Minerals (UK)	Iron Age	Journal of Commerce	Metal Bulletin (UK)	Metals Week	Minerals and Materials	Mining Journal (UK)	Northern Miner (Canada)	Purchasing World	Skillings Mining Review	Strategic Metals Intelligence
Antimony	●	●	●	●	●	●	●	●		●	●	●		
Arsenic		●					●	●		●		●		
Beryllium	●		●		●		●	●		●				
Bismuth	●	●	●			●	●	●	●		●	●		●
Cadmium	●	●	●			●	●	●	●		●	●	●	●
Cerium		●					●							
Chromium		●	●	●	●		●	●	●					
Cobalt		●	●		●		●	●	●		●			
Columbium			●				●	●						
Gallium		●	●				●							
Germanium			●		●		●	●						
Indium			●		●		●	●		●				
Iridium	●		●		●		●	●					●	
Lithium		●	●	●			●	●						
Magnesium	●	●	●	●	●		●	●		●	●	●		
Manganese	●	●	●	●	●		●	●	●	●				
Mercury	●	●	●		●		●	●		●				
Molybdenum	●		●		●		●	●	●	●				●
Osmium	●		●				●	●		●				
Palladium	●	●	●		●	●	●	●	●	●				
Platinum	●	●	●		●	●	●	●	●	●	●	●		
Rhenium			●				●	●						
Rhodium	●		●		●		●	●		●			●	
Ruthenium	●		●				●	●						
Selenium	●	●	●				●	●		●				
Silicon	●	●	●				●	●						
Silver	●	●	●		●	●	●	●		●	●	●	●	
Tantalum	●		●			●	●	●						
Tellurium	●	●	●				●	●		●				
Thorium		●			●									
Titanium		●	●		●		●	●	●	●				
Tungsten	●	●	●				●	●	●	●	●			
Uranium	●						●							
Vanadium		●		●			●	●		●			●	
Zirconium	●	●	●	●	●		●	●		●				

Developing a strategic metals price index

HOW TO INVEST IN STRATEGIC METALS
What Do All Those Different Prices Mean?

There are two basic prices for all metals. The one of primary concern to the strategic metals investor is the so-called "free market" price. The other is the "producer" price. The relationship between the two prices tells a lot about the supply and demand situation for any particular metal.

The producer price of a metal is the price at which a major producing company is currently selling the metal under long-term contractual agreements to large industrial consumers. It is convenient for both parties to do so because it provides the mining and metal producing firm with a guaranteed market for its metals. It also benefits the consumer because he knows his metal costs in advance and can plan his production and marketing accordingly.

Everything was hunky-dory until the 1970s when the cost of energy began to escalate, setting off rapid inflationary trends throughout the world. Almost simultaneously nationalistic and "liberation" trends in the Third World moved various governments to nationalize mining industries, while the Soviet Union and China became more active in worldwide metals trade, creating new markets and sources of supply. As a result the large producers found themselves in competition with a rapidly growing metals trading community selling the same metals at the so-called spot or free market prices. However, the majority of metals trade is still performed under the producer price system.

When there is a shortage of a particular metal the free market price moves up over and above the producer price and remains higher until production of metal catches up with the demand. Once adequate supplies come on stream the free market price falls below the producer price. As such the relationship between the two prices is a good indication of future demand and supply conditions and gives an advantage to the knowledgeable strategic metals investor.

The trend is toward more free-market pricing of metals, and many large producers are either abandoning or periodically not posting producer prices for some of their metals. The investor through his strategic metals broker is primarily buying and selling in the free-market, although when the producer prices are lower and producers are willing to sell there is no reason why the broker

WHERE TO FIND STRATEGIC METALS PRICES

should not take advantage of this opportunity. The investor may want to know, however, at which prices his metals are being bought for him in order to have an idea of a realistic value of his metal in the current market.

The best way to keep informed is to subscribe to one of the services or periodicals that regularly publish producer and free market dealer prices. Several such services are available, though at a significant cost. The small investor who keeps only $10,000 or so in strategic metals will probably find the cost prohibitive, but to the serious investor who wants to know what the metals traders are doing this service is a must.

What Daily Price Quotations Are Available

There are a few services that provide immediate price quotations by telex or telephone for many of the metals. These are designed for metals traders and consumers who may even write their contracts based on these prices. Most of these services are associated with specialized metals publications and their prices are widely quoted and used throughout the world. These services are provided by *American Metals Market, Metal Bulletin, Metals Week,* Commodities News Service, and Reuters.

American Metals Market has a Price Information Service that supplies metal price changes by telephone or telex for a nominal fee. This daily newspaper primarily reports producer prices for base metals but also handles dealer prices for many other metals.

The *Metal Bulletin* of London provides a special MB Digest service by telex that lists metal price changes on Mondays and Thursdays. These are then published in the *Metal Bulletin* on Tuesdays and Fridays. The MB Digest lists at least thirty different metal prices but is designed to be read with the bulletin itself and is available only to the subscriber. It costs about $450 per year plus transmission costs.

Metals Week has the Price Notification Service, which is sent by telex on a weekly basis late on Friday afternoons before *Metals Week* goes to press. *Metals Week* collects at least twenty-nine strategic metals prices. The cost of this service is $376 per year for one price and $22 for each additional price. Transmission charges are extra.

Commodity News Service offers an "MSN" Metals News Service for precious and nonferrous metals traders, dealers, and brokers. This service includes prices and news coverage pertaining to metals and is available twenty-four hours a day through a teletypewriter.

Reuters carries bid and asked prices for a number of strategic metals that are provided daily by certain brokers. Reuters also provides its own "London Free Market Metals" prices through its teletype network.

This last service, which was initiated only recently, is probably the most useful to the strategic metals investor. If its price quotations are used by brokers it stands to reason that investors will have to check those prices rather than any other. Although this service appears to provide a central price collection and information point, trade in strategic metals takes place on an individually negotiated basis and prices arrived at in such negotiations may differ considerably from those quoted either by Reuters or any of the various publications.

Weekly Price Reports Are More Readily Available

The most practical price quotations available to the strategic metals investor are published in the *Metal Bulletin* of London and *Metals Week* of New York. Both are relatively expensive trade periodicals and each carries the prices of about thirty metals. What makes them particularly useful is that for many strategic metals both periodicals quote producer as well as free market (also known as dealer or merchant) prices.

In addition, the prices of some of the metals are also quoted in several weekly trade periodicals such as *Chemical Marketing Reporter, Iron Age, Mining Journal, Northern Miner,* and others. Many of these are often available in the science and technology departments of larger public libraries, engineering libraries of colleges and universities, and corporate libraries of engineering firms. You can locate a sample copy and decide whether you wish to subscribe to any of these journals.

Chemical Marketing Reporter quotes the prices of twenty-two strategic metals or metal compounds of significance to the chemical industry. *Iron Age* carries the prices of twenty-one strategic metals that are of importance to the iron and steel industry. You would want to read their comments if you are involved in trading ferroalloys.

Prices of metals and metal ores are also quoted weekly by *Mining Journal,* from the United Kingdom, and *Northern Miner,* published in Canada. The disadvantage of some of their price quotations lies in the fact that many prices are given in pound sterling or Canadian dollars, giving you the additional task of currency conversion. The price quotations of *Metals Week* are presented uniformly in U.S. dollars and pound sterling for all metals. *Metal Bulletin* predominantly publishes prices in U.S. dollars or British pound sterling, but also includes quotations of metal prices at different world locations such as Belgium, Italy, or Japan. In such instances the metal prices are quoted in local currencies. If on top of being a strategic metals investor you would like to engage in international metals arbitrage speculation, then *Metal Bulletin* is for you.

Monthly Prices Appear in Specialized Periodicals

The average investor is unlikely to be involved in the strategic metals trading business so frequently that he would need to obtain weekly price quotations. There is also another reason monthly average prices may be sufficient to indicate trends. Prices of many strategic metals do not change from day to day. Many of the weekly prices quoted by *Metals Week* carry effective dates when they were last changed and in many instances weeks or months may elapse between such changes. In the case of some producer prices the amounts may remain fixed for years.

As a result the monthly average prices are quite useful and the most accessible publication for this purpose is the *Engineering & Mining Journal* published monthly by McGraw-Hill in New York. The E/MJ monthly, as it is known, carries the monthly average prices developed during the preceeding month by *Metals Week,* which is also a McGraw-Hill publication. An additional bonus in this magazine is a wealth of information about new mining discoveries and progress in mining throughout the world.

HOW TO INVEST IN STRATEGIC METALS

E/MJ quotes prices of twenty-five strategic metals and has a separate section for ores and concentrates and ferroalloys. Other monthly periodicals that carry prices of some strategic metals include *Purchasing World, Minerals and Materials Survey, Economic and Energy Indicators of the National Foreign Assessment Center,* and *Industrial Minerals* of the United Kingdom, which is a sister publication of *Metal Bulletin*. None of the above present as convenient a roundup of monthly average prices as the E/MJ magazine. The *Minerals and Materials Survey,* published monthly by the U.S. Bureau of Mines, quotes average or representative prices for eight strategic metals as well as all basic metals and some nonmetallic minerals.

Long-Term Price Trends Are Carefully Logged

The *Minerals and Materials Survey* actually publishes a long-term price series every month for chromium, cobalt, manganese, molybdenum, palladium, platinum, tin, titanium, and tungsten. Monthly representative prices are presented for the last two years, while the preceding ten years are covered on an annual average price basis.

The U.S. Bureau of Mines presents a long-term price series for most strategic metals in each of their individual metal brochures that are available from the U.S. Government Publication Office. Check Chapter 15 for details and addresses of various publications.

Several of the daily, weekly, and monthly publications also publish yearbooks with metal prices for the preceding year or longer. Perhaps the most useful to the North American investor is the *Metals Week Price Handbook,* which is published each spring and contains prices of nonferrous metals for the previous year. These yearbooks are available with prices going back to 1972.

For the statistically minded and computer-oriented, *Metals Week* has a computerized data base containing historical time series for all metals prices and exchange rates quoted over the years by *Metals Week*. It is updated weekly and may be accessed through the Interactive Data Corporation international time-sharing network.

WHERE TO FIND STRATEGIC METALS PRICES

Make Sure You Are Looking at the Right Price

If you are overjoyed by this wealth of price data on strategic metals, wait until you have had a chance to check all these sources out. There are prices, and prices, and prices, aside from the producer and free-market prices mentioned previously.

It would be nice if all these sources presented the same prices for the same metals, but they don't. The reasons are valid enough. The various publications cater to different industries, all of which deal with the same strategic metal but in different forms, shapes, and purities.

For the purpose of investing and trading in strategic metals it is best to stick to the prices of a metal form that is most commonly traded regardless of its purity. Ferroalloys in particular are traded in numerous compositions. Ferrochrome may come with chromium content ranging from 36 percent to 73 percent and prices are usually per unit of contained chromium. This is also true of various strategic metals ores that may be sold to you instead of pure metal.

By looking through those price quotations you will realize that giving an order to buy tantalum is not enough. You have to be more specific than that and decide whether you want it in rods, sheet, powder, tantalite ore, or even scrap. The price of each form of tantalum will vary, although it will generally be linked to the amount of tantalum contained in your purchase. Make sure your broker is aware that you know what those prices are all about and you won't get stuck.

chapter 9
The Laws That Affect Strategic Metals Trade and Use

Strategic metals trade is an unregulated business and there are no exchanges where these metals are traded. The volume of this trade, while growing rapidly, is relatively small and as a result there is little prospect that a formal exchange for most of these metals will come into being in the foreseeable future. On the other hand, abuses and fraudulent sales have already prompted federal and state agencies to act.

Other regulations, however, do affect the mining, smelting, trade, stockpiling, and consumption of strategic metals indirectly. They include foreign investment and production controls, export and import duties, environmental restrictions, health and safety standards, export controls, municipal and local warehouse restrictions, and possible price controls during periods of national emergency.

Watch Out for Fraud in Strategics

Fraudulent sales of tantalum scrap as high-grade electronics metal at inflated prices, and illegal sales of investment contracts for other metals, prompted state and federal authorities to investigate several strategic metals sales operations. Some arrests have already been made while other "boiler rooms" discontinued their operations, but the strategic metals investment industry received a terrible reputation in the process.

All these developments and simultaneous national strategic

THE LAWS THAT AFFECT STRATEGIC METALS TRADE AND USE

minerals policy issues also captured the attention of the U.S. Congress, where a number of committees began looking into strategic metals problems and are demanding action.

The House Commerce, Consumer, and Monetary Affairs Subcommittee has already asked the Securities Exchange Commission and the Commodities Futures Trading Commission to define the regulations governing the sales and speculations in strategic metals. As you know, there are none if strategic metals are sold outright for cash.

The House Government Operating Committee is investigating potential speculative bubbles in strategic metals and their impact on U.S. defense policy and expenditures. They are particularly concerned with chromium, cobalt, and titanium.

The House Select Committee on Aging has held hearings on off-exchange boiler room operations and is considering special hearings on strategic metals trading. This gives you an idea of who gets stuck the most.

The Commodities Futures Trading Commission has asked attorney generals of all fifty states to assist in cleaning up fraudulent strategic metals trading firms in their states. CFTC asked for information about specific boiler room operations and has already investigated a number of organizations in Florida, Texas, and California. The commission is also preparing a "spotters guide" itemizing telltale signs of fraudulent off-exchange operations to help banks, Better Business Bureaus, telephone companies, and other firms in identifying and reporting abuses.

All these activities will go a long way towards cleaning up the strategic metals business, but it will be some time before any significant regulations, if any, come into play. Private investors now and in the future must look out for themselves. The best way is to keep informed about individual metals prices, where they have been, and where they are going. Refer to Chapters 10 and 11 to get the details of what you should do before you invest.

How Foreign Regulations Affect Strategics

Various forms of taxation and restrictions on investment in foreign mining projects may affect sources of strategic metals from foreign countries. Canada, for example, is reviewing its mining investment laws in order to give the government more control over the industry. One of the proposals includes the creation of a federal Canadian nonfuel minerals marketing agency. Such a development would slow down the United States capital investment in Canadian mining. Similar effects could result from the Canadian government's direct participation in mining ventures. Canadian developments are particularly important because Canada appears to offer the greatest opportunities for the discovery and exploitation of new, secure sources of some of the threatened strategic minerals.

Australia, which calls itself the "lucky country" because of its abundant mineral resources, is also developing domestic policies designed to increase local processing of minerals to enhance their export value. South Africa, of course, has already succeeded in concentrating a lot of ferroalloys production within its borders. Sooner or later other countries will move to tax or even ban exports of ores, demanding that you buy refined metals or even products. If they have it and we need it that is what we will have to do, but the prices are bound to go up.

Import and Export Duties and Controls

One way in which the governments of the Third World countries can increase their revenues is to slap an export duty on their minerals. This is a popular measure because the taxation affects not their own population but only foreign exploiters. As nationalism grows and economic conditions do not improve, expropriation, nationalization, and taxation increase and eventually drive new investment away. Sooner or later this results in reduced production and even shortages.

By the same token consumer countries try to relieve such foreign taxation by lowering or even eliminating import duties on critical minerals and metals from certain countries. For example, U.S. Customs does not exact any import duties on the hafnium, indium, antimony, arsenic, cadmium, selenium, and bismuth that are imported from many Third World countries.

At the same time the United States uses its import duties to protect domestic industry and friendly foreign sources of supply from dumping or manipulation. Titanium, for example, from the

Soviet Union faces a very high rate of duty (25 –45 percent of its value) while titanium products from other countries are taxed at the 7–18 percent level with lowest rates applying to minerals and metals imported from the Third World countries. Cobalt, interestingly, can be brought in free of duty regardless of where it comes from, even the Soviet Union.

So it does matter where you buy your metals if you plan to import them into the United States. But there is another U.S. Customs regulation that might prove useful to strategic metals investors who want their metal stored in America. You can keep your metal in a U.S. Customs–bonded warehouse for up to five years without paying any duty whatsoever as long as you do not want to "land" the metal for domestic consumption. That sounds perfect in case you decide to reexport to some other place where they need it badly and it has appreciated in price, but you must keep in mind regulations affecting export controls and trade embargoes.

Environmental Regulation

From an investment point of view environmental regulation has done wonders to the prices of strategic metals. Keep in mind that automobile pollution control legislation created a whole new market for platinum, palladium, and probably rhodium in the future.

There are other effects, not too obvious at first glance, that also benefit the strategic metals investor. Environmental restrictions were responsible for the closing of several zinc-processing facilities in the United States in recent years. Domestic capacity is down to 50 percent and imports went way up. But zinc production is vital to the production of cadmium, germanium, indium, and thallium, which are zinc by-products. More future reliance on imports of those strategics seems in the cards, and that may mean higher prices.

The same can be said for copper. Major smelter and refining capacity is not coming on stream while demand keeps going up. More significant is the fact that arsenic, cobalt, rhenium, palladium, platinum, selenium, and tellurium are by-products of copper.

The effect of environmental restrictions and loss of productive capacity has a different effect on national security questions and there are those who now call for reexamination of the stockpile inventories in light of these latest developments. Any resulting decision may have significant impact on strategic metals markets and prices.

If the stockpile contains chromium and manganese ores and domestic ferroalloy processing capacity has been dwindling, there is a need to get rid of those ores and replace them with their respective ferroalloys. After all, what good are ores if you have no capacity to process them into the ferroalloys?

These are all environmental factors that influence strategic metals trade and prices, and the investor must be alert in advance about their effect. Likewise relaxation of restrictions may develop more domestic supplies and depress the markets. None of those effects are rapid, however, and an informed investor should have ample time to react.

Health and Safety Standards

The objectives of health and safety regulations are to ensure the welfare of those employed in the production and use of metals that have toxic effects. Mercury, lead, beryllium, arsenic, cadmium, and thallium are all highly poisonous substances. Other metals or their compounds are also toxic. Health and safety regulations are often linked to environmental controls when the toxicity affects the environment as well as the health of human beings.

Restrictions on the use of lead in paints and high octane gasoline have already resulted in reduced production of lead, which is often coproduced with zinc. The resulting loss of processing capacity directly affects the sources of lead and zinc by-products, which, as mentioned previously, consists mainly of strategic metals. More recently, restrictions on production and use of beryllium have also been having an effect on the few remaining producers of that metal in the United States.

Keep an eye on the Occupational Safety and Health Administration (OSHA) and new safety rules coming into play, as well as federal funding of research in order to eliminate the use of toxic substances. For example, breakthroughs in lightweight batteries made from synterials may pull the carpet from under the lead and

THE LAWS THAT AFFECT STRATEGIC METALS TRADE AND USE

antimony industries because both metals find extensive use in all car batteries.

Tax Incentives and Advantages

It may well be that in an attempt to mobilize private capital and promote a form of strategic stockpiling in the private sector, Congress may pass legislation providing special tax incentives for investing in and warehousing of strategic metals. It is almost certain that any such incentives would pertain only to metals held in warehouses under United States control, but such a development would set off a real boom in strategic metals.

Otherwise strategic metals are simply a hard asset that incur a maintenance cost that is probably deductible in most cases. You can really do well if you can get a loan from your friendly banker using your metals as collateral because the interest is also deductible. Individual investors must check their local state tax laws to find out if property tax is due, but it may be possible to avoid that by keeping your metals in a warehouse located in an appropriate state.

What a National Emergency May Do to Strategics

Investment in some strategic metals is sometimes justified on the basis of their critical need in case of a wartime emergency. The basic idea is that if you own a strategic metal its price will skyrocket when there is a real crunch, making you an instant millionaire or an influential figure overnight, admired for your vision.

The problem with this piece of fiction about strategics is a lack of understanding by an average investor of what such a strategic emergency means in real life. There is such a thing as profiteering, you know, and it is simply not going to be permitted when it involves strategic metals vital to national security. In times of a real national crisis during wartime, democratic institutions, human rights, and other peacetime luxuries are thrown out of the window and martial law takes over.

There will probably be compensation, but do not kid yourself about being able to bargain with the government about how much you want for your metal. Should you have it and the war effort require it, Congress will pass the necessary legislature to relieve you of it in such a hurry that you will not even have time to check the latest price.

This question has already occurred to some thoughtful strategic metals investors and they have hit on a happy solution: keep your metal out of the country and they can't get at it. Where? Why, in Rotterdam of course, the metals warehousing center of the world. The added attraction there is the fact that it is a London Metals Exchange–approved kindergarten for fledgling American strategic metals investors. You can simply buy or sell your metal there by sending a telex or picking up a phone.

Just how naive can you get? In the event of an emergency, a simple decree that citizens who hold strategic metals must turn over their warehouse warrants to the powers that be according to some "aid-to-the-enemy-if-not" act will take care of your metals in a foreign haven. Even if Congress was reluctant to be so harsh the Russians would probably reach Rotterdam in a couple of days after they decide to move and the whole issue would become academic.

Part 2
Mechanics of Strategic Metals Trading

chapter 10
How to Buy Strategic Metals

Calling a toll-free telephone number that you have seen in a newspaper and sending in the money is not the way to buy strategic metals. Calling several toll-free numbers to find out who will quote the best price for some strategic metals is a much better idea, but in order to play that game you must know what you are talking about. This chapter is designed to take you step by step through the motions.

Of course you may contact an investment broker or a financial planner with whom you have been doing business and ask him about strategic metals. Chances are he will tell you to stay away from this type of scam. He is right to want to protect you, but by doing so he may prevent you from getting a better return on your investments and having a hell of a lot of fun in the process. If you stay away from the boiler rooms and bucket shops you should be able to find a reliable source of strategic metals and take advantage of the opportunities. After all, the potential for profits in strategics is very big, so you might as well accept a little more risk than you would normally.

Make Sure You Have Sufficient Assets

Strategic metals investing is not for everyone, simply because the minimum investment is relatively high, on the order of $10,000. Why? The investment is dictated by the fact that you can buy and sell only certain minimum-size commercial quantities of each metal. Somehow these seem to be worth about $10,000, whatever the metal, give or take $1,000 or $2,000. *Don't* buy a smaller unit —it will be offered, quite legally, but it is illiquid.

This limitation by and of itself suggests that unless you have liquid assets worth at least $100,000 you should really stay away or look at strategic metals funds. You can buy five troy ounces of rhodium, the minimum commercial quantity, for around $3,000, but that's about it. You will then have one strategic egg in a basket, with little possible diversification. The minimum contract price of another metal would be about $5,000 for a quarter metric ton of vanadium. Most other metals are more expensive for minimum quantities.

If you have liquid assets of $100,000 or thereabouts, you can allocate 10–25 percent of those to strategic metals, but no more. However, with $25,000 you can now get into three metals such as cobalt, chromium, and iridium, all of which look very good as far as future potential for being unavailable. Future unavailability is good news for strategics investors.

The nature of strategic metals is such that quick profits should not be anticipated unless you invest at the outset of a periodic price escalation. As a result, you should be prepared to tie up your $25,000 for three to five years, because if you came in at the end of those peaking cycles that is how long it will take before they start increasing in value again. The more metals you hold, the more chance you have to catch a peak or two with an average appreciation of 400 percent, and that is a powerful incentive to keep your money locked up in strategics. The prices are creeping up anyway; every three to five years there are jackpots to be had.

You should not commit any funds that you may require for any other reason or an emergency. Strategic metals trends point upward over the long term but periodic fluctuations in price are very violent. If our investigation is to be believed it appears that you may have to prepare yourself for a long period of relative inactivity if you buy your metal at the wrong time. Chances are, however, that after three to five years you will hit the "peaks" and your metals will appreciate significantly. The important thing to remember is patience. If you can not keep your funds in metals for that period of time, you may not be able to catch that big move in one or two of your metals. This is important because just one of such moves will more than offset any inaction in other metals you hold and make the whole game worthwhile. It is admittedly an educated gamble.

It's a Cash Buy, No Futures, and No Margins

There are no exchanges, no terminal markets, no regulation, and no options to buy. This is not like trading commodities or gold, silver, platinum, or palladium on margin. Strategic metals are a cash buy and you have to take delivery. This is one more reason why you should have only those assets in strategics that are not required for daily living or business expenditures.

By the same token you should stay away from anybody who offers you strategic metals on the basis of a down payment that would appear like a margin in a futures market. The Commodity Futures Trading Commission (CFTC), which regulates trading in futures, does not have jurisdiction over sales of commodities for cash. Strategic metals are relatively small markets, at least half of which are no larger than $100 million per year on a worldwide basis. Such thin markets do not justify the existence of formal exchanges as is the case with copper, aluminum, nickel, zinc, lead, and tin, for which futures contracts are traded at the London Metals Exchange and can be accessed by registered commodity brokers.

Precious metals including gold, silver, platinum, and palladium are also traded on the New York Commodities Exchange (COMEX) and the New York Mercantile exchange. Commodities brokers can get you in and out of futures for those metals. It is also true that platinum and palladium can be considered very strategic and indeed they are. If you have a feeling about those, then there is no reason why you should not call your investment broker, who will get you in and out of those metals with the greatest of ease and will let you buy on margin if you like.

The confusion sets in when someone who is or was a commodities broker enters strategics. You may have been used to getting your margin from him and may even ask about it. It is very hard to resist a customer who is eager to buy and needs a little push in the form of a margin because he does not have the capital necessary to pay for the minimum contract.

The broker may also try to talk you into pooling your inadequate capital with similar amounts from other customers who also can not afford to get in on this good thing. Be careful. Unless your share can buy at least the minimum commercial quantity of the strategic metal in question, stay away from such a scheme. There is a valid reason why a broker may want to pool your funds with those of others who want to buy the same metal. If he shops around for a larger than minimum quantity he will probably get a much better price. Remember that these are negotiated markets and each transaction takes place individually. The more he buys the cheaper it is to you and the less commissions he has to pay. That is fine as long as you get at least the minimum commercial quantity of any metal you purchase.

This is not to say that commodities pools in strategic metals do not exist. They do, but unless they are offered by a registered commodities broker have nothing to do with them. You will be dealing with securities in a regulated market. If you must enter a pool, stick to taking delivery and getting your very own warehouse receipt for at least the minimum commercial quantity deposited in a bonded warehouse and insured by Lloyds of London. And make sure that the warehouse receipt is in your name. They will tell you that leaving it in bearer form makes for liquidity, but warrants get stolen, and having it in your name is just an extra precaution. Insist on it.

Choosing the Metals to Buy

Many of the chapters in this book discuss the various approaches and criteria that you can use in choosing which metals to buy. It would be nice if you were able to peek into the holdings of some of the strategic metals mutual funds and trusts that are coming into play, but secrecy usually surrounds these matters. Nevertheless, you can also improve your batting average by concentrating on groups of strategic metals that may rise and fall jointly because they share common or overlapping markets and end-use applications.

The thirty-odd strategic metals that are worth bothering about fall into distinct groups, and your choice may be made easier by dealing with each group at a time. You may concentrate on a few metals within one group or pick the most promising from each group to make up a selected portfolio. We are specifically talking about the ferroalloys metals, the superalloys metals, the electronics metals, the electro-optics metals, the catalysts, the nuclear metals, and so on. Many metals fall into more than one group and as such are particularly interesting from the investment point of view, as shown in Figure 12. It is a little like spreading your risk at the consumer end.

There are also other groupings applied to strategic metals, based on certain common characteristics. These would form the ferrous metals, the refractory metals, the hard metals, etcetera, but such groupings are less market-oriented and do not offer any advantage over other approaches.

The ferroalloys metals account for at least 60 percent of the global production of all strategic metals and are clearly important by virtue of an overwhelming position in the marketplace. They include manganese, silicon, molybdenum, chromium, titanium, tungsten, vanadium, tantalum, and columbium, and also nickel, which is one of the basic metals. Ferroalloys fortunes rise and fall with the steel industries of this world. Just keep in mind that steel industries of the West are in decline while steel industries of the communist countries and the Third World are expanding. Nevertheless markets are sizable, mostly over $100 million for each metal.

The superalloys metals are the high technology aerospace materials for jet engines, missiles, satellites, rockets, nuclear weapons, reactors, and modern plants. Some of the ferroalloy metals are also major superalloy metals, but cobalt has been king in this lot. Because it is so important it will always have a use in superalloys, but those who do not control cobalt sources of supply will do their best to substitute nickel, tantalum, or anything else. The superalloys are still big movers but relatively smaller quantities of metals are sold for superalloy use than for ferroalloy consumption in the steel industries.

The electronics metals are the darlings of them all. Not only are their names exotic—antimony, gallium, germanium, rhodium, ruthenium, and tantalum—but their markets are smaller, demand for them increases faster than that of the economy in general, and supplies are not very elastic because most of those metals are

Figure 12: **Major Strategic Metals Groups**

Major metals group	Typical metals	Market size range
Ferroalloys Metals	Manganese Silicon Molybdenum Chromium Titanium Tungsten Vanadium Tantalum Columbium	$100–$4,000 million
Superalloys Metals	Cobalt Titanium Tungsten Tantalum Columbium Molybdenum	$50–$2,000 million
Electronics Metals	Arsenic Silicon (crystal) Antimony Gallium Germanium Rhodium Ruthenium Gold Tantalum	$25–$300 million
Electro-Optics Metals	Antimony Cadmium Gallium Germanium Indium Tellurium Iridium Selenium Silicon (crystal)	$10–$300 million
Catalytic Metals	Platinum Palladium Rhodium Iridium Rhenium	$25–$1,200 million

by-products of the basic metals like copper, zinc, lead, and nickel, whose production may be static if not actually in decline. That's good. These are growth metals, in demand by a growth industry. Go get them while they last.

The electro-optics metals are the metals of tomorrow and more often than not also electronics metals. This is the world of infrared warfare, sensors, detectors, fiber optics, lasers, high technology weapons, solar power, and supertelecommunications. Some of the markets are thin but may explode tomorrow, adding to the demand created by electronics. If a metal is important in both electro-optics and electronics you probably have a winner.

The catalytic metals are extremely interesting because of their unique properties. Petroleum refining and emission control are the most obvious uses, but the scientific community is only now embarking upon a more systematic approach to the study of catalysts. We know that only the most inert metals can do the job because all others would react with the chemicals of the process. This means platinum, palladium, rhodium, iridium, osmium, ruthenium, and rhenium. It also means extreme scarcity, very inelastic demand due to extreme by-product relationships, and traditionally high prices. In addition these metals have a high degree of portability because you can lock them in your safe. This lot looks very good indeed.

What Are the Selection Criteria?

Whether you want to evaluate all the strategic metals for your own satisfaction or only those suggested to you by your broker, there are a number of selection criteria you should apply to check them out. Remember your broker may have just gotten a quantity of some metal in a distress sale, and he wants to get rid of it at going prices because his profits will look very good indeed. Check the fundamentals, and keep in mind these change with time. What was true about a metal a year ago may not be true today, and that glossy promotional brochure is not always up to date.

We have identified fifteen independent criteria in Figure 13 that you should use in trying to make your decision. You can also ask your broker what he thinks about the metal he is trying to interest you in with regard to those criteria. This will give you an opportu-

Figure 13: **Selection Criteria**

1. Above-average growth industries applications
2. Significant markets of $100 million or more
3. Limited substitution potential for each metal
4. Ease of storage and portability
5. Few sources of supply
6. Political action vulnerability
7. Cartel potential
8. High by-product dependence on a basic metal
9. Frequent price action history
10. High energy requirements for production
11. Strategic, industrial, and investor stockpiling
12. Mutual funds and trading interest
13. Regulatory restrictions
14. Recycling potential
15. Financial and tax incentives

nity to check whether he is keeping track of what is going on or is simply pushing a metal or two because it is coming to market in great quantities.

1. Ask yourself if the metal in question is being used in the industries growing faster than the economy in general. Electronics would certainly qualify under this criterion, but even in electronics there are some sectors that are literally exploding while more mature sectors may stagnate or may even be going out of fashion. High technology industries have a very high rate of innovation.

2. Look at the size of global markets for the metal that interests you. Figure 5 in Chapter 3 is your guide to their relative production volumes and markets. The bigger the market the more liquid your investment in such a metal will be. By the same token it will not fluctuate as wildly in price as those with relatively thin markets.

3. If there are no substitutes for the metal, that's a good short-term indication of future price increases. But if the supplies are also disrupted too often, you can bet that someone is hard at work on substitutes or product redesign to eliminate its

use. Lack of substitutes today does not guarantee a demand for the metal tomorrow.

4. Precious metals of the platinum group are ideal from the investor point of view because they can be easily stored and are readily portable. Other metals are highly toxic and dangerous and present unusual storage and handling problems that make them undesirable as investment vehicles. Arsenic, beryllium, cadmium, and magnesium fall into this category. Unless there are unusual reasons to invest in those you should probably eliminate them on this basis.

5. The fewer the sources of supply of a metal, the greater the probability that shortages may develop and prices will explode. This is a result of the ease-to-control production as well as the lead time necessary to bring new sources of supply on stream when there is a sudden upsurge in demand.

6. Geopolitical considerations are paramount when it comes to those strategic metals whose sources are predominantly in foreign countries with unstable or even hostile governments. They have it and we need it and they know it: It's as simple as that. Sooner or later they will do something about it. Cobalt is the classic example, but antimony, chromium, columbium, manganese, platinum metals, tantalum, vanadium, and tungsten are all vulnerable to political action and produced in only a few countries.

7. Cartels in non-oil minerals and metals cannot last, say the experts, and they are right. But during the short-lived attempts you have an opportunity to make a lot of money, which is what cartels are all about. Remember that in many Third World countries the distinctions between mining enterprises and governments are nonexistent. Evaluate in conjunction with point 6 above and the major concentrations table (Figure 3) in Chapter 3.

8. By-product dependence is an important factor that makes for inelastic supply of a metal. In general the big volume ferroalloy metals are mined in the form of ores but most of the

HOW TO BUY STRATEGIC METALS

others are by-products of copper, nickel, zinc, lead, and even gold production. By-products of by-products such as rhodium, iridium, and ruthenium are therefore even more dependent on the basic metal supplies.

9. Price volatility varies with different metals. Aside from distinct peaks every few years showing price increases of several hundred percent, metal prices fluctuate on a short-term basis. Some, however, have been very flat and stable for years. You will probably want to get into those that fluctuate.

10. Energy plays a vital role in mining, refining, and transportation of all metals. Energy requirements vary vastly from one metal to another and will influence the cost of production. Rising energy costs will generally assure a rise in metal prices but at some point reprocessing and recycling processes that use less energy will come into play and flood the market with metal from secondary sources.

11. Stockpiling effects are an important influence, and worsening global tensions may drive more governments toward this action, creating shortages of the most critical metals in Japan, western Europe, and the United States. Germany, France, the United Kingdom, Sweden, Italy, and Spain are known to be considering or planning national stockpiles, but the actions of the United States National Strategic Defense Stockpile overshadow them all in size and variety of metals in the inventory. Industrial stockpiles are very important influences on trade and prices, so watch their levels. Investor stockpiling is a new activity but may become a force in selected strategic metals.

12. The advent of strategic metals mutual funds is bound to have an effect on some metals. Try to figure out what they are holding and buying and stay ahead of their game. If these funds show profitable operations the professional metals trading community may get into it in a big way and a global strategic metals roulette will become the greatest game in town.

13. Imposition or easing of environmental restrictions on mining, smelting, or even use of certain metals will continue to

affect their consumption and supplies, but these vary from country to country. Evaluate their impact on the industries in which your metal is of importance.

14. Recycling potential, as previously discussed in Chapter 5, must be considered as an alternative source of many strategic metals. This potential will increase as the prices go up. Look for growing applications of strategics where their use is so diffused that recycling is impractical.

15. When interest rates are high new mine financing suffers and this will be reflected in future shortages and higher prices. Tax incentives in various forms to promote mining would have the opposite effect, but it takes up to ten years to bring a new mining project on stream. On the other hand, tax incentives to stockpile could pull a lot of metals out of circulation and create artificial shortages and price escalations.

Beware of Minimum Trading Units and Acceptable Metal Purity

Strategic metals and all other industrial metals are traded in certain standard quantities that are convenient to consumers and generate commission to metal traders. These standard quantities are such that normal transactions represent minimum dollar values in the range of $50,000 to $100,000 and often considerably more. To a metals trader the amount of time and effort required to transact a $100,000 trade is practically identical to that involving $10,000 or less. As a result traders prefer to deal with large industrial clients, who also get the best prices in return for buying larger quantities of metals.

The standard or average industrial trading quantities are about five to ten times larger than the minimum commercial units of each metal and may consist of lots made up from convenient numbers of minimum commercial units. A list of minimum units can be found in Figure 14. It stands to reason that a trader who is negotiating or expecting to sell a standard industrial lot to a commercial client of long standing is unlikely to be interested in breaking it up because a strategic metals broker from Minnetonka found an investor in Paducah who wants to spring for a quarter

Figure 14: **Minimum Trading Units and Metal Purity**

Metal	Minimum commercial trading units	Standard industrial trading quantities	Maximum available purity	
Antimony	2–5 tons	10–50 tons	99.5–99.6%	
Arsenic	1 ton	5 tons	99.5%	
Beryllium		1–5 tons	99.0%	
Bismuth	1 ton	1–5 tons	99.99%	
Cadmium	1 ton	5–10 tons	99.95%	
Chromium	1 ton	5–10 tons	99.5%	
Cobalt	0.25 tons	1,5,10 tons	99.9%	
Columbium	1 ton	5–10 tons	99.5–99.8%	
Gallium	50 kilograms	100 kilograms	99.999%	
Germanium	5–20 kilograms	100 kilograms	99.999%	
Indium	25 kilograms	100–500 kilograms	99.97%	
Iridium	10 troy ounces	100 troy ounces	99.90%	powder
Lithium	1 ton	10 tons	99.9%	ingot
Magnesium	5 tons	20–100 tons	99.80%	ingot
Manganese	5–10 tons	100–500 tons	99.70%	
Mercury	15 flasks	50–100 flasks	99.99%	flask
Molybdenum	0.25–1.0 tons	10 tons	57–60%	oxide
Osmium		25–50 troy ounces		
Rhenium	50 troy ounces	50–100 kilograms	99.9995%	
Rhodium	5–10 troy ounces	100 troy ounces	99.90%	
Ruthenium		50–100 troy ounces		
Selenium	0.50 tons	1–5 tons	99.90%	
Silicon	10 tons	5,10,100 tons	96–99.7%	
Tantalum	0.05 tons	1–5 tons	99.90%	
Tellurium	0.25 tons	1–5 tons	99.70%	
Titanium	0.25–0.50 tons	5–10 tons	99.60%	
Tungsten	1 ton	25–50 tons	99.95%	
Vanadium	0.25–2.00 tons	10 tons	83.00%	oxide ore
Zirconium		5 tons	65.00%	oxide ore

Source: Compiled by Geostrategics, Inc.

of a ton of titanium. That is worse than no deal at all because the metals trader has neatly stacked up five- to ten-ton lots of titanium for his clients and is not going to mess that up for you. This is so even though a quarter-ton of titanium is an acceptable minimum trading unit. The point is that your broker has to find a metals trader to whom this minimum trade is acceptable, not the other way around.

Minimum commercial trading quantities, even though they are considerably smaller than standard industrial lots normally traded, are perfectly acceptable in metals trade. The prices are simply not as advantageous as those for the larger quantities.

However, quantities of metals that are smaller than the commercial trading units are almost unsalable, regardless of how much demand there is for the metal. The investor, therefore, should make absolutely sure that he is buying a quantity that is at least the minimum commercial unit.

The problem is that some unscrupulous brokers or traders may agree to sell metals in units smaller than the minimum commercial quantities and may even do so at inflated prices. The investor must familiarize himself with the size of the minimum commercial units of the metal he wants to purchase and never agree to anything else.

If you have more than the minimum amount of capital required for such an investment, you may do well to purchase a standard industrial lot that consists of a multiple number of minimum commercial units. Not only will you get a much better price for the metal but should it appreciate significantly in price you can then recover your capital by selling some of the minimum commercial units while continuing to maintain a position in the metal. However, such an investment would only be possible with a minimum outlay of at least $50,000 to $100,000, and you would also want to obtain separate warrant receipts for each of the minimum commercial units that comprise the standard industrial lot of your metal.

The other point to watch is the purity of the metal you are buying. Each metal comes in various forms such as ingots, broken cathodes, powders, or even ores, and each of these forms may be refined to a different purity level. There are certain minimum purity levels that make a metal acceptable for trade and you should always seek the highest purity available.

Figure 14 shows the maximum purities of metals traded. Note the very specific purities of such metals as gallium, germanium, or rhenium. When the purity acceptable to an end-user in industry is specified as 99.9995 percent, this is exactly what is desired. Do not let anyone talk you into accepting the same metal at 99.999 percent purity as equivalent. The five ten-thousandths of a percent *does* make a difference, particularly in the case of electronic, electro-optical, and catalytic metals.

Theoretically every metal can be further refined to the desired purity, but only at a cost in energy. In order to obtain that extra fraction of purity the energy required may be much larger than that needed to refine the same metal to a lower purity. The significant difference in price for metals with seemingly similar purities that differ by only fractions of a percent may very well be justified by that extra energy input. The worst that can happen to the unwary investor is that he may be charged for the highest grade metal while being delivered lower grade material. After all, tantalum is tantalum, they may tell you, but the fact is that tantalum can be high-grade electronics metal or scrap, and you had better know what you are paying for.

Finding a Reliable Strategic Metals Broker

Now that you have a definite urge to get into strategic metals, where do you buy them?

This question boils down to finding a broker, and it is no good looking in the Yellow Pages under "strategic metals" because they have not yet caught up with such a category. In frustration you may end up with a boiler room that makes itself known by aggressive advertising.

Let's just define once again what we are looking for: A strategic metals broker is someone who buys strategic metals from professional metals traders on your behalf. He gets a commission for knowing which metal traders will sell minimum commercial units. That's about it.

What is stopping you from going directly to the metal traders? Nothing. If you are a serious investor you should develop your own contacts. You can identify the metal traders throughout the world by going through the sources of information described in Chapter 15.

If you are an average investor with only the minimum investment amount to spare, then the broker makes sense. But the strategic metals broker is in a new profession, unregulated, without a track record, and herein lies the problem of finding out his reliability.

Ideally you are looking for a professional metals trading organization that is also selling strategic metals for investment purposes. There is only one such firm in the United States at present: Bache Halsey Stuart Metals, a subsidiary of the Bache Group, a well-known investment brokerage house and now also a subsidiary of the Prudential Insurance Company. This firm has been in the business of metals trading for thirty-five years, so they are professional insiders, so to speak. In 1981 they also began offering a selection of about twenty strategic metals for public investment and are developing a diversified metals mutual fund as well. You may not elect to buy through Bache, but you owe it to yourself to check their prices and get their opinions.

The other investment and commodities trading firm that is well known in the investment community, primarily because of its trading in precious metals during the 1970s, is the Sinclair Group. In early 1981 this company formed the Strategic Metals & Critical Materials, Inc., specifically for the purpose of investing in strategic metals, and could be considered the first strategic metals broker in the United States. Although this firm had considerable experience in trading precious metals and other commodities, it has not been involved in industrial metals trade per se for as long as the Bache Metals Company. Both companies, however, offer strategic metals primarily to investors who are interested in developing metals portfolios of $100,000 or more.

All other brokers are basically imitators of those two companies, and of the Strategic Metals Corporation in London, which is described in more detail in Chapter 13. Some are registered commodities brokers but others are just precious metals trading firms or only unregistered and unregulated firms selling strategic metals. As long as you buy physical metal from them for cash there is nothing illegal about it.

Perhaps your best bet when dealing with an unregistered broker is to ask for references. A reputable broker should be willing to give you the names of people who have bought strategic metals from him. You can check with a few such buyers to find out how quickly they received their warehouse warrants after sending in their checks. You can also ask the broker to tell you which metal traders are his suppliers. It may be worth your while to check with those traders to find out if the broker follows through promptly in paying for the metals he orders on his client's behalf, because that determines how quickly you become the owner of the metals you purchase through him. If the broker is reluctant to give you such information, try someone else.

If you do not have the time or inclination to look for a strategic metals broker yourself, put your investment broker, accountant, financial planner, or even banker to work on this question. He may charge you for this effort but it could turn out to be money well spent if he can produce a list of strategic metals brokers and recommend one or two for your consideration. Without being personally involved, such third parties are always in a better position to give you impartial advice. He may even be in a position to act as your broker, and if you have a well-established relationship and confidence in his judgment, your search is over.

What to Ask the Broker of Your Choice

Once you've narrowed your selection to one or two brokers with whom you plan to do business, you should check them out thoroughly before you hand over your money. The problem is, some may be so new that they have no track record to speak of. Nevertheless, you should find out as much as you can about his knowledge of the strategic metals game. If you read this book and he did not, chances are you know more about it than he does.

Assuming you are satisfied with his financial responsibility, capitalization, references, and his reputation in your community, the time has come to find out more about his business and knowledge of strategic metals.

A good start is to ask the broker for his home telephone number. Tell him you are very busy during the day and you would like to call him after hours to chat about strategic metals informally. After all, geopolitical developments affecting strategic metals occur day and night all over the world and your investment is not a trivial one. If you come across an event through your profession or as a result of foreign travel you may want to take advantage of it immediately. Perhaps you could even invite him out for a drink to meet him and size him up. Strategic metals is a relatively illiquid commodity, not unlike real estate. Would you buy a house without meeting the real estate broker face to face?

Once you have made contact you should find out whether strategic metals is the only investment product or one of many handled by the firm. If your broker also handles stocks and bonds, commodities, futures, gold and diamonds, real estate, mutual funds and money market funds, he must have a significant staff to do a good job, or else he is just a commission salesman. Ask him if he spends his full time on strategic metals or other investments as well. There is so much happening in strategic metals that it is a full-time job just keeping track of developments.

A strategic metals expert in a larger organization is backed up by an established business base that provides cash flow and keeps the enterprise afloat. A small firm dealing exclusively in strategic metals is operating in a new, highly competitive market and has a negligible track record. Unless it is well capitalized to enable it to last for a year or longer without making a profit it may disappear from the scene very rapidly. Ask about capitalization of a new firm, and try to find out who the principal owners and investors are.

Find out as soon as possible how the broker handles your money. The proper way to do it is to have an independent customer trust account in which your funds should remain until the warehouse warrants arrive showing that the metal has been purchased. On receipt of such warrant the trustee, which is usually a bank in your community, releases your money to the broker. It is like putting your money into escrow pending satisfactory completion of all documentation when buying a house. The existence of a third-party customer trust account is an incentive for the broker to execute your order promptly. Otherwise he is tempted to keep a large "float" and live off the interest on your money.

Ask the broker whether he recommends molybdenum as an investment and why. This is a tricky question and will quickly tell you how well he knows his strategic metals. If you have read this book this far you know that the United States controls over 60 percent of all molybdenum production in the world. It is not critical to us and is not in our strategic stockpile. But it is very strategic and critical to Japan, western Europe, and most other countries. As a result they are stockpiling it, and foreign metals brokers include molybdenum as one of the major strategic metals in their portfolios. Many of the new American brokers have simply imitated the British brokers, obviously without doing their own fundamental thinking about molybdenum.

Actually there was a sharp increase in the price of molybdenum in 1980, but this immediately resulted in increased supplies that indirectly led to price reductions. It is a tradeable metal with a large market, so it is not to be completely discarded as an investment. You can watch how the few domestic producers control that market while you are making a profit. Let's see how much your broker knows about it.

In order to test his integrity in the metals business, ask the broker if he sells futures, options, or other financially leveraged plans in strategic metals. If the answer is not an emphatic "physical metals for cash only," pay for the drink and leave at once. There is no likelihood of a strategic metals exchange in the conceivable future and any options available abroad are not legally traded in the United States. Any suggestion of buying strategic metals "on margin" is a danger signal. Stay away.

Once the broker has passed all these preliminaries you might want to ask him for more details about how he buys and sells the metals. Remember, even at this stage there are good and bad ways of doing business and staying afloat. And you should worry about him staying in business at least until such time that your warehouse warrants arrive, which in the extreme case could be 180 days—six months!

This is the time to ask about minimum commercial quantities and whether or not he could sell you a smaller amount. Or perhaps you could pay as you go, buying small amounts of a strategic metal until you collect the commercial unit of minimum size. *In either case he should firmly refuse to do so.*

You should also ask about your broker's sources of strategic metals. One reason is to get a reference about his business discipline, but you also want to know if there may be some closer relationship between him and a particular metals trader. If the broker buys large quantities of a metal for direct resale to investors at a profit, the liquidation of his inventory is probably more important to him than objective investment in strategic metals. Find out from the customers and the broker if he appears to be "putting people into indium" and nothing else, or whether he executes orders for various metals. Ask him, in fact, how many different metals he has handled in the last month or two and with how many metal traders he is doing business.

By the same token you should ask the broker whether he is an agent for a metal producer in the United States or abroad. That could prejudice his judgment. You do not know what incentives there are for the sale of one metal rather than another when you are dealing with an agent. If the broker deals with metal producers as well as with metal traders or merchants, he should be dealing with several and not be locked into a single source.

This leads to the question of prices. Ask the broker how many sources he checks for the best price when he executes your order. This is a problem because for some strategic metals there are only a few sources and some of these may not wish to trade in small quantities. Also, many of the metal trading firms, both independent and captive of large metal producers, are located in Europe. This means cross-Atlantic telephone calls, telex, and travel, all of which add considerable expense to a strategic metals brokerage operation. Ask the broker about prices but plan to develop independent sources of information once you purchase the metals, as described in Chapter 8.

All this affects the execution of your order. You will want to know how quickly the broker will act. If he tells you that "when circumstances require" he will delay execution, holding out for a better price for you, ask him to define the circumstances and put a cap on delays of execution. You do not want your money waiting six months for the proper circumstances while the broker collects the interest. By now you must have realized that you do not want to deal with a broker who does not have a customer trust account under third-party control.

When the sensitive question of commission comes up, if the broker tells you "none," look out. He has to eat, and one way or another you will find that between the time he buys the metal and the time you pay for it its price has gone up by 20 percent just because you bought it. That is acceptable—after all, you expect a greater appreciation over the long haul. But it also means that unless your metal goes up in price by at least another 20 percent, you will not make a cent if you have to liquidate.

Actually, only a part of the 20 percent goes to the broker. The remainder pays for warehouse costs, assays, inspection, and insurance costs, but the broker likes to collect all those expenses from you in advance if he can. When you throw in his commission, perhaps in the form of a "setup" charge that may come to a few thousand dollars, the 20 percent collective markup to the investor is a figure that is hard to get away from if you want to survive in this business.

Then there is the question of delivery of the metals you purchased because you have to take physical possession. There are three ways this can be accomplished and your broker should be able to handle them all. You may elect to have the metal shipped directly to store it in your safe or bank vault if it is one of the portable metals like rhodium or germanium. Or you may want it in a warehouse of your choice where you can personally inspect it, in the country where you live. In those instances you will have to pay for shipping in addition to all other charges. Or you can leave it where it is, which more often than not is a London Metals Exchange–approved warehouse in Rotterdam, the world center of strategic metals trade. Your broker should be in a position to arrange the alternative of your choice.

The broker may or may not be qualified to advise you on setting up strategic metals accounts for joint partnerships, corporations, pension funds, and trust accounts. This will depend on his background as a financial planner or accountant, but such investments should really be set up separately and the broker brought in only for the purpose of purchasing the metals. Most brokers would love to service such accounts because that means larger trades and commissions. On the other hand, depending on the nature of such group investments in strategic metals, he should be able to purchase metals in minimum commercial units for individuals participating in such schemes. This provides additional flexibility if one or more members want to liquidate or transfer their holdings.

When it comes to selling your metal, ask the broker on what basis is he willing to do it for you and what his commission will be. Actually brokers cannot guarantee that they will sell your metal because they do not make a market and there are no exchanges for strategic metals. The broker should, nevertheless, agree to accept your metals for sale on a "best efforts" basis, but since you are the outright owner you can sell them yourself at any price you manage to negotiate. Again, as with purchases, find out how quickly after the sale you will receive the proceeds and get a commitment in writing. You should also be free to sell your metals through any other broker, but make sure that you have your warehouse certificates in your possession and that they represent at least the minimum commercial units. Otherwise neither your broker nor any other will want to handle your metal.

How Much Commission to Pay

The strategic metals broker earns his living by buying the metal you want at a specific price from a metals trader or a producer and either charges you a set commission or marks up the price of the metal, which is equivalent to a commission. The question is, How much is a fair commission?

A good guide to the reality of strategic metals investing costs are the published fee schedules of the Strategic Metals Corporation in London. Many of the original American brokers took its schedules as a model, although some may have used different percentages.

In a nutshell, if you entered with the minimum investment of $10,000 to $25,000, you would be charged 13 percent of the total. This would include 8 percent as account-opening fee, 2.5 percent as purchase transaction commission, and another 2.5 percent payable at the time of purchase to cover the sales commission when you decide to sell. The explanation for the advance payment of the 2.5 percent sales commission is that this way you avoid a larger fee later when your metals increase in value. No one seems to remember that if your metals decrease in value you will be paying a much larger commission when you sell, while the broker collects interest on your prepaid sales commission as long as you own the metals. And what happens if you want to sell through another broker?

These investment costs drop dramatically to only 1 percent in account-opening fees and 0.5 percent in buy and sell commissions if you come in with $1,000,000 or more. But if you have a million to spare on strategics, you can probably do even better dealing directly with metals traders. On the other hand, if you have just

$10,000, the metals traders may not even care to talk to you. You need the broker and he socks it to you. Or does he?

Let's stop here and figure out just what a metal broker does get out of this. From an investor with $10,000 who pays the highest rate, the broker collects $1,300. From the millionaire the take is $20,000—only 2 percent of the million. Clearly most of the new crop of the strategic metals brokers selling to the small investor are not making maximum commissions, particularly when high interest rates on short-term securities are wooing away the big spenders.

Now look at the economics of operating as a broker for a year. Assume that a single broker sells one $10,000 account every week, bringing in $500,000 in cash for the year. If he kept 13 percent he would end up with $65,000 after one year of operation. Out of that $65,000 must come the overhead: the office space, marketing expenses, accounting, the paperwork connected with warehouse receipts, documentation, advertising, and all other business expenses. Let's not forget research, which he badly needs, particularly if he is competing to sell strategic metals for investment. That $65,000 based on 13 percent in account fees and commissions does not go very far. A small firm will probably have to spend 60 percent of that amount per man to keep going, leaving the broker with a salary of about $26,000 per year.

An analysis of several pricing schemes used by strategic metals brokers suggests that the industry is still searching for an equitable formula. Since the industry is not regulated it is every man for himself. One of the first American strategic metals brokers who followed the Strategic Metals Corporation pricing scheme and even jacked up the minimum investment fees to 15 percent could not make ends meet and went out of business. It stands to reason, therefore, that the strategic metals broker must be able to realize in form of fees, commissions, and other charges between 15 percent to 25 percent of the minimum investment or he cannot survive.

This is why brokers are seeking the larger accounts of $50,000 or more. With larger accounts they can drop the overall fees below 10 percent and survive with a much smaller number of accounts and customers. The trend in the industry is toward the emergence of brokers serving intermediate accounting, investment, and financial planning firms who in turn deal with either relatively wealthy individuals or with groups of people controlling larger sums of money. But for the individual investor, this only interposes an additional middleman between him and the metal trader. Even though the brokers may earn smaller commissions as a percent of their business, the individual investor will have to absorb the added cost of dealing with another layer of service. He will end up paying the overall 15–20 percent increase in the cost of metal as it moves from the metal trader into his portfolio.

Checking Out the Research Backing Your Broker

The field of strategic metals is relatively new and there is not much solid research available on the subject. Not that there is not a lot of information on strategics, but it has not been formalized into a specialized body of knowledge. As a result brokers are frantically searching for research capability to support their claims and recommendations, but few of them are aware of the costs involved in doing a proper job.

It takes about $1,000,000 in cost and many months of tedious research to trace the total supply and demand pattern for a single metal from mining through smelting, refining, trade, stockpiling, and consumption. Only the largest mining corporations can afford to engage in such effort, which is conducted by well-established research organizations, often on a multiclient basis. Even then individual participating firms pay from $15,000 to $25,000 or more for such a study and forecast for a single metal. Interestingly, whether the metal represents a large worldwide market or only a small one, the cost of thorough research does not vary very much.

Clearly the broker who is primarily a very small businessman cannot afford to conduct such extensive research and probably will not even participate in some of those multiclient studies. What he may be able to do in the future is to hire some of the marketing experts from the large metal-producing corporations or metal trading firms as advisors. Other experts such as geologists, mining engineers, metallurgists, or political advisors are unlikely to have the marketing and trading background best suited to untangle the mysteries of strategic metals trade. Economists and business types have little knowledge of strategic metals and high technology industries. The result of all this is that only the big multinationals *really* know what is going on.

Seeking Outside Advice

It is obvious that in the present state of strategic metals investment the broker does not have the resources to engage in any serious research to support his recommendations. His best sources of information are the metal traders and producers from whom he has to buy the metals. He can question just how objective their advice is since their business is sales and distribution of metals and not investment of assets for appreciation.

If you are a small investor risking about $10,000, you may not have much of an incentive to spend time researching strategic metals trade and prospects. Your best bet may be to invest in one of the strategic metals funds. Since they control large sums of money they can afford to allocate 10–15 percent of their profits to a good research effort (see Chapter 13). If you are an investor who puts at least $100,000 into strategic metals, you can afford to pay for research and advice and it may save you some money.

One example of the cost of keeping up with developments is this author. I must spend at least one day each week collecting all pertinent information for a comprehensive monthly digest on strategic metals. Competitive industry rates for such research and analysis run easily to $500 per day. That comes to $25,000 annually just to keep current on strategics! Any in-depth analysis of such data is extra.

chapter 11
Which Documents Are Important?

In the excitement of buying and selling strategic metals, investors are often not paying enough attention to the proverbial "small print" within their contracts with the brokers. Strategic metals, which become fully paid property on purchase, come with a certain amount of documentation and paperwork that must be handled properly to avoid problems at a later date.

Now that you have made the decision to become a strategic metals investor, take the time to understand the necessary documents that are required to establish and maintain your ownership. Keep in mind that your broker may be dealing with strategic metals suppliers and warehouses in one or more foreign countries. This means lengthy funds transfers, international travel, different national jurisdictions, and foreign languages. All of those factors can combine to make for very frustrating delays if the documents involved are not properly executed and promptly handled.

Confirmation of Purchase

The first document you are going to get from a strategic metals broker is the confirmation of the purchase of metal on your behalf. It should identify the metal, the quantity purchased, the minimum purity and form, and of course the price. So now you own the metal. Not quite.

What you do have is a receipt stating that you have transferred a certain amount of money to the broker. Now that he has the

WHICH DOCUMENTS ARE IMPORTANT?

funds he will order the metal you want from the metals trader, who in turn will contact a warehouse where the metal is stored and instruct them to issue a warehouse warrant or certificate. *Until you receive the warehouse warrants you have no title to the metal you purchased.* If you read the conditions of delivery carefully you will find that it may take anywhere from thirty days to six months before you receive your warrants. Until then you must hope and pray that your broker stays in business because he is your only link to your metal.

Client Trust Account

The most secure way to purchase strategic metals is through a broker who deposits your funds in a client trust account administered by a third party like a bank. The funds remain with the trustee until the metals broker completes the purchase and delivers warehouse warrants, purchase order, assays certificate, and insurance policy to the trust account. After the documents are received and found in order the funds are released from the trust account and payment is made. Ideally you should be sending your check directly to the trust account, which would instruct the broker to proceed with the purchase on receipt of funds.

Unfortunately this practice is not always followed by strategic metals brokers. In most cases they maintain one or more accounts in a bank into which your funds are deposited. Any interest earned in such accounts is usually kept by the broker. These are not independent trust accounts and are under the control of the broker.

If the purchase is international in nature payment may have to be made in a foreign currency. As a result of exchange rates fluctuation, the final purchase price and initial storage and insurance fees may differ from the amount of funds deposited by the investor originally, and small adjustments should be expected.

Warehouse Receipts or Warrants

The metals trader or producer keeps the metals he sells in a warehouse. In most cases it is a London Metals Exchange–approved warehouse in Rotterdam, the world center of strategic metals trade. Delivery of a purchased metal is effected by the issuance of a warehouse receipt or warrant to the new purchaser of the metal.

Strictly speaking, the investor could request to ship his metal to any other location rather than simply leaving it where it is and accepting the warehouse receipt. On the other hand, if the investor plans to sell his holdings at a future date, the fact that the metal is in an **LME**-approved warehouse in such a central metals market will generally expedite the sale.

The warehouse warrant is a receipt made out in the name of the owner or in "bearer" form, according to client instructions. The warrant is numbered and identifies the specific warehouse in Rotterdam where the metal is stored. In addition it identifies specific units of metal purchased by number and indicates the gross and net weight of the metal in kilograms.

The warrant also indicates the monthly storage fee per unit of metal in local currency and the starting date of storage. It makes clear that insurance of the metal is the responsibility of the bearer of the warrant and it gives the name and address of the warehousing firm.

Sometimes a metal for which a warehouse warrant is issued may be in transit to the warehouse. This may drag out the delivery period. Some brokers may also advise you to accept warrants in bearer form because this speeds up the process of delivery. This is hard to understand because it takes equally little time to type in a name or the word "bearer" on the warehouse warrant blank. However, if a bearer warehouse warrant is lost by a client, it becomes almost impossible for him to prove he owns the metal. Therefore you should insist on getting warehouse warrants in your name even if it does take longer. Once you receive your warehouse warrants you should keep them in a safe or a bank vault as a valuable title document.

The delivery of these warehouse warrants may take anywhere from thirty days to 180 days. The length of time required is explained by purchases of metal that is in transit or otherwise not readily available at the time of purchase. The storage costs are assessed monthly and are borne by the client. In most cases they are 0.25 percent of the value of metal. The payment for storage is billed to the client every six months.

WHICH DOCUMENTS ARE IMPORTANT?

From the point of view of the national security of the United States, warehousing of strategic metals in Rotterdam is questionable. In case of an outbreak of hostilities in central Europe, access to Rotterdam would quickly become impaired and the metals lost. The investor can ship his metal to any other warehouse, including bonded warehouses in the United States, where import duties do not have to be paid for up to five years. The cost of shipping is borne by the owner, and should you choose to do so your broker should be able to make all the arrangements.

Storage and Insurance

Although warehouse warrants are proof of your ownership of the metals, they also impose upon you the responsibility for storage and insurance of your holdings.

The storage and insurance charges are usually arranged by the broker as part of his service to you. In most cases they are in the order of 0.25 percent per month based on the current value of your holdings. This comes to 3 percent annually and you are billed every six months, more likely than not in advance.

The storage and insurance charged by various brokers during 1981 varied between 2.0 percent and 4.5 percent, but on the average ran about 3 percent per year. In one case an additional onetime storage documentation charge of $75 was also imposed.

Since the storage and insurance charges are computed monthly and based on current value of your metal it may be worth finding out who assesses their value every month and according to what price quotations. Find out if the charges are based on the metal price at which the broker purchased it from the traders or at the price that you must pay after all his commissions are figured in as well.

An interesting point here is what happens if the prices of metals decrease. Theoretically if your metal becomes worthless you can dump it in that warehouse forever free of charge, so clearly the warehouse must have a minimum storage charge, below which the cost of storage cannot drop no matter how low the price of metal falls. You may want to find out about that limit. After it is reached the cost of storage and insurance will quickly rise above the 0.25 percent per month that you thought you were paying.

London Metals Exchange–approved warehouses and Lloyd's of London insurance are what you want when you keep your metals abroad because these are the most reliable, well-established, and regulated institutions. Some brokers may try to shave a few corners by trying to talk you into accepting insurance coverage from other companies. You may save a few dollars or he may make a few more, but you're probably better off with a Lloyd's insurance policy.

Should you decide to store your metals in the United States, there are numerous warehouses available. If you are importing the metal into the United States from abroad and there are import duties on it you can keep it in a U.S. Customs–bonded warehouse for up to five years without having to pay any duties unless your metal is "landed" for actual consumption within the United States. The regional U.S. Customs service office will provide you with a list of U.S. Customs–bonded warehouses in your area, but whether these are LME-approved warehouses is another matter.

Your broker should be able to arrange the shipment of your metal from wherever it was purchased to the warehouse of your choice, in the United States or any other country. Clearly since this is an additional service optional to the purchase of metals, you will have to pay for the shipment and perhaps even an additional service charge. You may find it cheaper to instruct your broker to simply find a quantity of the metal you want that already exists in a United States warehouse.

Storing your strategic metals in the United States may be patriotic, but it does not necessarily add to the liquidity of your investment. This is so because Rotterdam and London are the main strategic metals markets, and there is some distrust among European metal traders about what American warehouse warrants really represent unless they are issued by an LME-approved and inspected warehouse. What this means is that when you want to sell your metal it will take your broker longer to do it, and he may not be able to get as good a price for it as he would if it were stored in Europe.

How Do You Know What You Have Bought?

This is a very good question. After all, you only have a piece of paper giving you title to a box, or a drum, or some other

WHICH DOCUMENTS ARE IMPORTANT?

package. It is in some warehouse in a city you have never been to, in a country you may have rushed through in a few hours during your visit to Europe. You take it for granted that the box exists because the warehouse warrant says so. But you wake up one night wondering what is in that box. Rocks? Sand? Or perhaps strategic metal scrap nowhere near the quality necessary for its use in the high-energy laser weapons that you are sure are going to revolutionize the strategic balance of the world.

The simple answer is that you do not know what is in your box in that warehouse. For that you need another set of independent documents that tell you what an inspector saw when he looked into that box. These documents consist of assays, sampling, and weight certificates, and are prepared by independent auditing firms. Only on the basis of such periodic documentation will the warehouse issue its warrants and the insurance company its policy.

There are firms that specialize in sampling and chemical analysis of materials stored in warehouses, and they provide this documentation, which is usually passed on to you free of charge by the broker. If the metal is purchased directly from a metal producer he usually provides a certificate in place of such independent assays, but if you are worried about the possibility of someone tampering with your holdings you may arrange for such periodic inspection on your own. It will have to be done anyway once you decide to sell your metal. Here again, although most brokers provide such documents as part of their services, some have been known to charge investors a onetime fee on purchase, amounting to $150 for assaying and another $100 for weighing certificates, so shop around.

One such sampling and assaying firm seems to be turning up repeatedly when strategic metals are purchased from brokers. If you are interested in ordering your own inspection, you may want to get in touch with them and ask about their services and fees. Their address is:

> DANIEL C. GRIFFITHS & COMPANY LTD.
> Perry Road
> Witham, Essex CM8 3TU
> England
> Telephone: (0376) 515 081
> Telex: 995281

The chemical analysis and sampling certificates are often combined in one document and performed by the same firm. Such a report identifies your metal and the date of inspection and gives the precise description of the container, its size, and condition, as well as your metal unit-identifying numbers that appear on your warehouse warrants. Make sure they are the same on both documents. The report also includes the gross weight of your consignment and the actual weight of the metal it contains. This information is used by the warehouse as a basis for calculating the value of the metal and the storage charges.

The sampling report includes a description of the form, color, size, and structure of your metal and may include remarks on how clean or how contaminated your metal appears to be.

The assays document is a chemical analysis report based on laboratory findings obtained when a sample of your metal was analyzed. Basically it indicates the purity of the metal contained in the unit and gives percentage composition of any impurities, identifying elements such as carbon, sulfur, and so on. The assay report is an important document, particularly if you are dealing with electronic, electro-optic, and catalytic metals.

After inspection of the contents the container is sealed by the inspecting firm. Once the seals are broken and your container opened the metal must be assayed again before it becomes a salable commodity in the metals trade.

Keep in mind also that with time metals may change their chemical composition, depending on warehouse conditions, even when they remain in sealed containers. Magnesium is particularly unstable over long periods of time. This is one reason traders insist on storage in London Metals Exchange warehouses, where certain standards of storage conditions are maintained, ensuring more stability.

Risk, Arbitration, and Force Majeure

Because of the risk involved and the relative illiquidity of strategic metals investments, many brokers want their clients to sign a risk acceptance form and a financial disclosure statement before transacting business. Read such documents carefully because they may give you some ideas about how a particular bro-

WHICH DOCUMENTS ARE IMPORTANT?

ker operates. This is where you will sign away your right to the interest on your money while it is sitting in the broker's account waiting for the "opportune time" to complete a purchase on your behalf.

The risk disclosure statements that you may also be asked to sign often require you to reveal fairly detailed financial information about the size of your assets, and warns you that the only appreciation in your metal that you can expect may come from an increase in its price and your ability to sell it at a future date. The important thing to remember if you sign such an agreement is that you absolve your broker completely from having to sell your metal in the future. To put it bluntly they tell you that once you own the metal you are stuck with it, and you are supposed to agree to it in writing. Clearly an honest broker will make his best efforts to sell your metal since that is his business, but keep in mind that no one is obliged to make a market in any strategic metals and they are simply making sure that you agree to that principle in writing.

Disagreements between brokers and investors in the strategic metals game are bound to take place because this is unregulated territory and everyone can play. Investors may make claims against brokers, warehouses, and assay companies for a multitude of reasons. If you have read the last few chapters, you realize that opportunities for abuse abound. This is also one good reason why this business will attract many unscrupulous operators. Until some regulation comes into play there is little the public can do about it.

Some brokers realize that disputes will arise and have a provision in their agreements to submit to arbitration. This is fine as far as it goes, but the strategic metals investment business already spans at least two continents and several countries. Find out in advance to which arbitration your broker will conform. It may not be the one that is appropriate to where your metal is.

Finally there is "force majeure." An important clause in minerals and metals supply contracts, it permits the parties not to fulfill their contractual obligations due to events beyond their control. Let's say your lot of germanium is in transit from Namibia and civil and labor unrest resulted in it's being hijacked into Angola. Do you get your money back? Does your insurance cover such a loss? Will your broker make good with a similar lot of germanium on its way from China? How long do you wait? Ask him about it and don't be surprised if he does not know what you are talking about. It is just an indication that you are both involved in something new.

chapter 12
When to Sell Strategic Metals

This is probably the toughest question to answer and at this stage of the strategic metals game it may even be academic. Why? Because if you are an investor who is interested in physical metal, you are buying, not selling. Everybody is buying, they tell you. If so, why don't they buy the metal you have for sale? Interesting question. You should have asked that before you bought.

But let's not worry about that now. You've got the metal—or a piece of paper from a warehouse operated by a firm with a delightfully unpronounceable Dutch name—and they have your money. You call that toll-free number to find out the latest price and find that the number is discontinued. You have no idea what the price is. That's illiquidity.

Price histories of most metals show sharp peaks in each metal every few years, suggesting that some price action or shortage took place that increased the price several times within a very short time. You could almost say that if you hold some of the more active metals long enough you simply can't go wrong, because sooner or later you will be swept up automatically when the action comes.

If this is so, then the ideal position of an investor is to be able to identify the price surges in one metal after another and simply move in at the start and get out at each top within a year or so. Perhaps this is the theory that the new strategic metals mutual funds and trusts managers are hoping to put to the test, because the opportunity appears to be there.

The cobalt shortages and price escalations of recent years are considered by some to have been caused by informal producers' action under the price leadership of Zaire. Cobalt certainly continues to present significant cartel potential, and the recent formation of the Cobalt Development Institute in Helsinki suggests that producers are getting more chummy and serious about the future of their metal as substitution efforts among consumers intensify.

Titanium metal has also gone up in price significantly in recent years, supposedly triggered off by Soviet withdrawal from the markets. But it also appears that titanium metal producers in the United States engaged in some form of price-fixing and made several titanium consumers mad enough to undertake antitrust action. One titanium expert claims that titanium prices move in cycles of three to four years. Look out for the next one.

Antimony may be another candidate for cartel action in the future. The first international antimony producers meeting has been scheduled by Bolivia in La Paz in September 1981. Prices of antimony have been in decline for some time and South Africa announced a 33 percent production cut earlier in the year. But it will take Bolivia, China, South Africa and the Soviet Union, who jointly control 70 percent of antimony ore production in the world, to perpetrate an effective cartel in that metal. They may not want to sit at one table together, but this does not mean that they will not follow the price leadership of one or two major producers among them. Such an informal cartel can be very effective in the marketplace for a short time, and that is when you have to recognize your opportunity.

If you look at the free market price history of most strategic metals during the last ten years or so you will discover that many experienced very significant and short-lived price "bumps" that occur almost regularly every few years. During each period of such price escalations several strategic metals are involved almost simultaneously. This becomes most dramatic when you record these bumps on a time scale, as we have done for you in Figure 15.

When only very sharp price escalations of 100 percent or more during a one- to two-year period are recorded over the last decade, the result is a series of peaks for specific strategic metals. For example, during the 1969–1971 bump period antimony, selenium,

Figure 15: **Periodic Price "Bumps" of Strategic Metals**

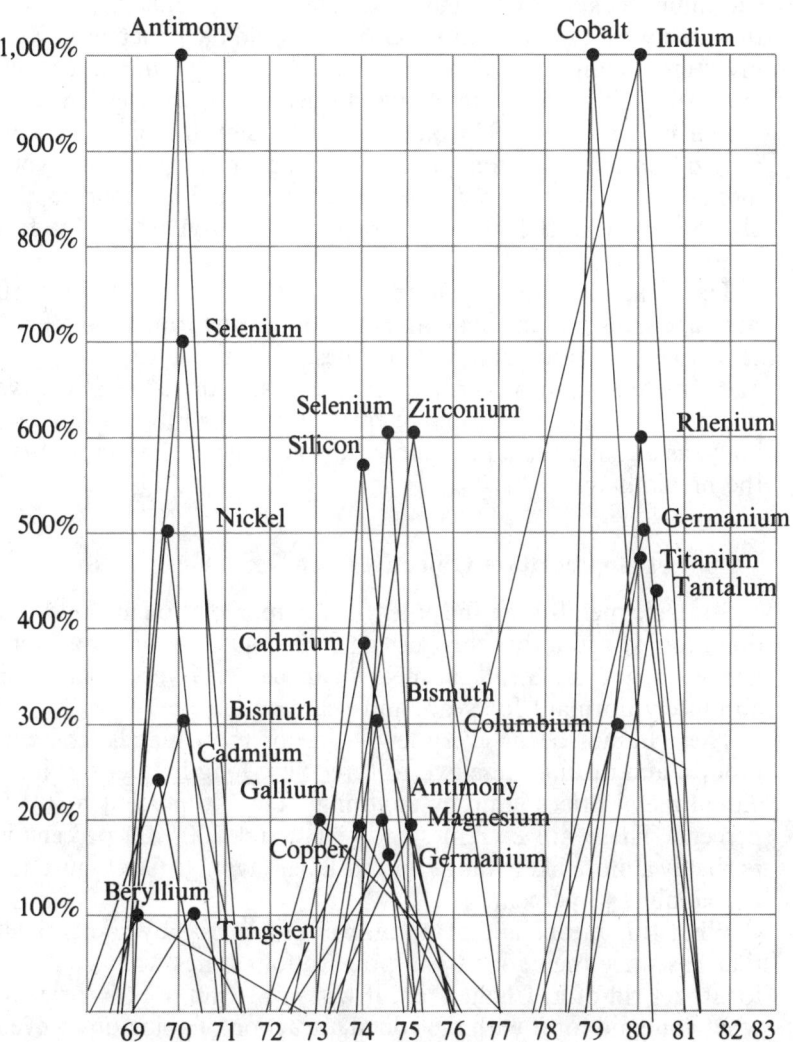

Increase in peak price of metals

cadmium, nickel, bismuth, and, to a lesser degree, beryllium and tungsten were the star performers. You could have increased your investment tenfold if you were smart enough to get into antimony and at least doubled your money in beryllium or tungsten.

During the 1973–1975 bump period bismuth, silicon, selenium, zirconium, and zinc gave you a chance to quadruple your money. But antimony, cadmium, magnesium, gallium, and copper also gave a 100–200 percent appreciation if you feared the fast action.

The next collective upsurge occurred during the 1979–1980 period, during which cobalt and indium outperformed the others, each rising in price almost ten times. Cadmium, rhenium, germanium, tantalum, tellurium, titanium, and tungsten also gave you an opportunity to triple or quadruple your money. Interestingly, as a group the latest bumps appear to have risen more than the previous ones.

Set Appreciation Objectives but Don't Get Greedy

Strategic metals have the potential for appreciation in value, but don't fool yourself that this goes on forever just because your rent and groceries do. Strategic metals can be very, very volatile or absolutely dormant for years and years on end.

These bumps occur every few years for most metals, come in groups, and during these two-to-three-year-long hot periods individual metal prices jump by anything from 100 percent to 1,000 percent. These are extremes, however, and 200–400 percent is probably a more likely range for most. The average (see Figure 15) is roughly 440 percent.

What this means is that if you were lucky to buy some metal that has since then gone up in price to four times what you paid for it, get rid of it. Chances are it will now drop back in price to what you paid for it with the added attraction of going down even faster than it went up. Of course, it may continue going up, but the odds are against you. During the ten-year period of our analysis ten out of twenty-six metals peaked in price temporarily by over 440 percent. Only three out of twenty-six, or slightly better than 11 percent, increased over 700 percent in those peak periods. Half of the metals never really made it above 300 percent. In a way

WHEN TO SELL STRATEGIC METALS

you have a fifty-fifty chance of tripling your money if you catch one of those bumps at the start.

Tripling your money in two or three years is equivalent to somewhere near 75 percent compound interest for two years or a very healthy 45 percent or so if you have to wait three years for it—not bad.

Chances are, of course, you will not be able to catch the metal at the bottom of a bump and ride it all the way up till it triples in price, so don't get greedy. Set yourself an objective such as doubling in price, then get out. After all, that is still very much better than the best of all the money market funds, and you may have a few other metals left in your portfolio.

Logically, it could be expected that the next runup of metal prices is likely in the 1982–1985 time frame, but the trick is to find out which metals. Chances are most of the aerospace strategics will be affected because military and high technology demand will be coming into play significantly then, while the output of basic metals and their strategic metal by-products may still continue sluggish as a result of economic slowdowns, recessions, and high inflation rates. This suggests that if you can get into a strategic metals fund as soon as these become available, opportunities to cash in on those forthcoming bumps will be very good indeed.

Get Ready for the Rollercoaster

What happens if you invest in a single metal at one of those peaks because everybody else seems to be doing it?

You'll get a ride all the way down faster than they can do the paperwork and send you those warehouse receipts that prove you own the metal. Who cares? You paid for it up front, and until your check clears those metal traders will not deliver any metal to you. Now, if you were a big spot buyer and knew the game you could perhaps negotiate a spot price at delivery time yourself. As it is you are too small a buyer to worry about.

The point is, if you are investing in one metal only you can very well do it at the wrong time and feel that you are stuck with a pile of scrap after it drops in price several times in a hurry. The question is: How long before another peak?

The rapid price bursts of 100 percent or more do not happen

every few years for every metal. They seem to occur simultaneously for several metals but not necessarily for the same metals every time. But do not despair. The long-term trend is quite definitely up, and unless much cheaper synterial substitutions are discovered for your metal the trend will continue. The real problem is that the long trend *is* long. Cobalt rose 750 percent in price from 1979 to 1980, but during just a slightly longer period of 1979 to 1981 cobalt only appreciated 100 percent.

Now germanium is peaking, tripling in price from $300 per kilogram in 1977 to over $1,000 in 1980. What to do?

The first thing is probably to find out where it stands on the price-supply curve. It may be nearing the upper boundary, above which it would have to be gold or platinum with all the monetary psychology behind it, which it is not. But it *is* a critical metal in all those electro-optical systems and there is not much of it around. The market is thin. It has nowhere else to go but up. Right? Wrong . . . probably.

Remember how germanium was big in electronics when everybody was using germanium transistors? Ever thought about what happened to all that electronics scrap? Somewhere somebody is sitting on a very big pile of scrap germanium of electronic grade and is waiting for a price that will make it worthwhile to extract the germanium. When that happens that germanium price will just tumble down so fast you won't even know it happened. Come to think of it, if germanium is so critical and strategic why don't we have it in the strategic stockpile?

Identify the Pertinent Geopolitics Affecting Your Metal

Let's look at those strategic metals that come from only a few politically unstable countries where revolutions abound. Surely those must offer opportunities for price escalation because their supplies can be cut off without warning.

That's quite true, but the nature of one political upheaval is not the same as that of another. One day there may be a more pronounced move to the Marxist rule and nationalization in Zimbabwe, and chromium prices may go up. If you catch it at the outset you are doing fine.

WHEN TO SELL STRATEGIC METALS

Then Jonas Savimbi may start a real civil war in Angola, get the South Africans to help him, and take over the country, pronouncing a capitalist regime. That's nothing to worry about. Angola is not a major producer of any strategic metals today.

But suddenly Savimbi allows Angola to be a base for expansion of his political philosophy to Zambia and Zimbabwe and the South Africans are helping him, threatening to start exploding nuclear mines if the Americans or the Russians came anywhere near. They take over Zambia and Zimbabwe, hang the socialist and Marxist leaders, and proclaim capitalism. Farfetched? Perhaps, but not impossible. The important thing is what happens to the price of chromium, which will suddenly become abundant all over the place. You have to think about it in advance and try to react as soon as the geopolitical developments take place.

No one has the time or opportunity to keep an eye on political developments throughout the world. The assassination of a Sadat in Egypt is worldwide news, but the escape of the prime minister of Zaire to Belgium only rates a few lines on page seventeen of a very few major newspapers. Who cares about a palace revolution in some steamy tropical country where people wear funny clothes and do not speak English?

You should, because that seemingly insignificant event is much more important to the world of strategic metals. Particularly if the deposed minister, like Karl-I-Bond of Zaire, gets immediate political asylum in Brussels, threatens to start a revolution to depose Mobutu, the tyrant of Zaire, and shows up in Washington a few months later, meeting with U.S. officials, businessmen, financiers, and who knows who else.

This is just one of the more recent events. So much is happening on the geopolitical scene all the time that it is impossible to figure out the effect on your metals of all that is going on. You can, however, narrow down your interest to those countries that are in a position to influence the supplies of the metals you are interested in and affect their prices. Chances are those countries lie along the famous global arc of instability, more specifically in central and southern Africa. Go back to Chapter 3 to identify which metals are mainly produced in which politically unstable countries and watch developments in those that affect your metals.

Have Your Paperwork Ready and up to Date

All those good ideas about the right time to sell your metals are worthless if you cannot immediately transfer the necessary documents once you have a buyer. This means warehouse warrants, insurance certificate, assay reports, and sampling certificates. If all you have is a confirmation of your purchase from your broker, you're not ready to sell unless your broker is still there and willing to take it off your hands.

Remember when you buy strategic metals that the broker promises to deliver the full documentation to you anywhere between 30 to 180 days from the day you send him a check. At about 15 percent interest in an average money market fund the $10,000 or so you give him will cost you $750 after 180 days. Think about it. Unless you receive ownership pronto you are paying for not owning the metal. What kind of a deal is that? Insist on getting your warehouse warrant in the shortest possible time or find another broker.

Don't get conned by talk about exclusive sources. There are several major traders for each metal and all the brokers have to go to one of them. You might as well pick the one who gets the paperwork done fast and will not bank your money, earning himself interest while you supposedly wait for documentation to come through. So keep that paperwork all together and handy when you are planning to sell. Otherwise you may find you do not own anything because you cannot prove it and your broker may not be there anymore.

Check Out Metals Brokers Who Will Buy on the Spot

There are not many strategic metals brokers who will buy your metal on the spot unless you are willing to accept only a fraction of what you paid for it only a few days ago.

In the case of a strategic metal currently in demand, a broker still requires a few days to find a buyer. Chances are that the price will not change dramatically, if at all, during that short period of time. You will also pay commission on the sale of your metal, but since you own it you have the privilege of shopping around for the best offer.

WHEN TO SELL STRATEGIC METALS

The point is, the time to check the brokers out is not when you want to sell but before you buy. You do not have to go back to the same broker when you want to sell, so line them up in advance and tell them what metal you hold. Remember, now you are also a source. If things move up and demand is brisk they will call you up to find out if you would like to sell. If by then you have realized your 200–300 percent price appreciation over two to three years, give it to them. Check for the best offer and let them have it. You've survived another peak. Now watch the prices tumble and get back in for a fraction at the bottom.

Keep in Touch with End-Users—You May Save Their Skin

An ambitious dentist who invested in a ton of nickel called the vice-president of purchasing at Allegheny International, which is a major user of nickel, cobalt, and other metals. The dentist wanted to sell his ton and take the profits. It was explained to him that the company spills a lot more than that when they put the nickel in the furnace. They could not be bothered with what to them was a drop in the proverbial bucket.

On the other hand, a major oil company spent a lot of executive time and effort chasing only half a ton of rhenium all over the country—no producer had that much in stock. Would you have made out if you had offered your fifty ounces, the minimum commercial quantity? Probably not. You'd still be a drop in that particular bucket. But that sort of news gets around in the metals trade, and you would have been able to sell your rhenium at a very handsome profit and let the brokers get stuck with it.

This illustrates that industrial use of strategic metals is no joke, but you are if you're an average investor. The quantities you are holding are peanuts in comparison with consumption, and if you throw it into the Hudson river out of frustration it will not be missed and national security will not be jeopardized. Keep your sense of proportion and be realistic.

This is not to say that in your vicinity or state, or indeed the country, there are not end-users who would be happy to buy your rhenium, rhodium, or ruthenium during a crunch. But they don't know you exist if you don't tell them about yourself.

Find out who uses the metals you hold in the quantities you

have and let them know about it in advance. They may get into a bind and you may be at the right place at the right time. Of course, keep in mind that if your metal is too far away, in Rotterdam or western Samoa, that may not be practical either.

There is another bonus that comes from keeping track of what the end-users are doing. They may develop new uses for your metal, which you will know about in advance. Don't count on your broker to tell you that. He is so busy chasing prospects and doing paperwork that, no matter what he tells you about keeping up to date, he simply does not have the time. He is a follower most of the time of what the metal traders want him to believe. Wouldn't it be nice to lead him by the nose for a change, telling him what to buy and when to sell and making a profit all the time? You can do it if you put your mind to it and let the brokers just do the chores of buying and selling for you, for which they get their rightful commission anyway.

The end-users are the original "bad guys" in the metals business because they are constantly scheming to substitute metals with cheaper materials. If you keep in touch with them, offering your metal for sale, you may be the first to know that it is being phased out from some use. Tough luck. But the end-users will also tell you about new uses if there are any and how important these may become. Keep in mind that the end-user is no particular friend of the metal trade people and may have been stuck in the past with an outrageous price hike or inadequate allocation quota during a shortage. He can sympathize with you rather than your broker or your metals trader. Use him when you can.

Do Your Own Research If You Can

This is crucial in order to spot the trends and, more specifically, the price peaks of strategic metals. Many brokers and even traders will tell you that there is practically no information about strategic metals. This is not true. There is a great deal of information available for the asking, if only you know where to look.

The brokers, who work on a rather thin margin, and the journalists, who rely on what they are told, have neither the time nor the background to dig up the information about strategic metals

WHEN TO SELL STRATEGIC METALS

geopolitics, markets, substitution, and new uses. At best they can get the latest available prices and pass them on to you, more often than not relying on rumor to explain the price movements or lack of them.

Because you as an investor are only involved in one or a few metals at a time you can do much better than that. In the last chapter of this book we have identified all the sources of information about strategic metals that are available to you. You will see there are many and most are quite accessible. It helps if you live in New York, London, or Washington, but even in remote areas you can subscribe to just a few pertinent publications and know more than your broker.

Nevertheless, recognizing the fact that strategic metals information, although readily available, is greatly diffused, we have created the *Strategic Metals Intelligence* monthly digest to help you out. It compiles all the latest developments about strategic metals investments, funds, markets, stockpiles, geopolitics, conferences, and publications in one package.

Strategic Metals Intelligence is not for everyone. It is designed to objectively present all the factors that affect the trade. As such, it is not a broker's newsletter, pushing one metal or another. It candidly tells you both sides of each story. It is expensive, but its $500 per year subscription may save a serious investor much more than that. For the readers of this book we offer a special introductory subscription at 10 percent off the regular price. Write to me and tell me that you read about it in this chapter. If you would like a free sample copy contact:

BOHDAN O. SZUPROWICZ
President, 21st Century Research
8200 Boulevard East
North Bergen, NJ 07047

If you are wondering about research on strategic metals, then this digest will make it easy for you. The *Strategic Metals Intelligence* digest is a monthly summary of the most important findings of our research, and it will keep you as current as your broker, many of whom are also our subscribers.

HOW TO INVEST IN STRATEGIC METALS

Don't Forget the Tax Breaks When They Come

Selling a strategic metal even at a loss may be of use to you in order to offset other capital gains on your tax return and will be treated as sale of property. The warehousing, insurance, assays, and sampling costs are clearly deductible because these are necessary to maintain your metals.

Some of the new strategic metals funds may offer a feature whereby a bank will give you a loan of up to 50 percent of the value of your strategic metals holdings. The interest on such a loan would be tax deductible, much like interest on a house mortgage is, since it is your property. If your metals happen to appreciate in value by 100 percent or more, as well they might, such a loan would let you have your original capital investment back without paying tax, while you would still own the metals that would provide the collateral for the loan.

Depending on future legislation with regard to strategic metals and minerals, it is not unlikely that tax incentives may come into being that will provide opportunities to further profit from the purchase and sale of strategic metals. Keep an eye on developments on this front since the government may want to encourage the private sector to assist indirectly in exploration, mining, pollution control, conservation, stockpiling, substitution, and trade in strategic metals. Individual objectives and financial positions will differ, however, and you should consult your accountant, financial planner, tax attorney, or even the IRS about tax regulations applicable to your specific case.

Part 3
Investment Alternatives to Direct Ownership of Strategic Metals

Chapter 13
How about a Strategic Metals Investment Fund?

Why not? With all the problems and pitfalls of individual metals investment, a professionally managed metals fund seems the obvious answer.

Lack of liquidity, large capital outlay, cumbersome paperwork, and scarcity of information on strategic metals are the major reasons that keep the average investor wary of plunging into strategics by purchasing individual metals. If, in addition, an investor would like to spread his risk and buy a portfolio of about ten of the most attractive strategic metals, he would have to come up with about $250,000 in capital. Clearly the strategic metals investment game in this form is not for the junior league.

Do not despair, because help is on the way. The investment community, always attuned to the whims of those with discretionary income to spare, recognizes all the stumbling blocks to more popular strategic metals investing. Eager to cash in on the strategic metals concept, the investment community has brought out the old standby of minimum risk investment (the mutual fund idea) to help you out.

It's an Idea Whose Time Has Come

The strategic metals mutual fund in one form or another is one idea whose time had arrived almost as soon as strategic metals brokers began peddling individual metals to small investors. See Figure 16 for some types of funds.

Figure 16: **Types of Strategic Metals Funds (October 1981)**

Name of fund or trust	Minimum investment	Current status
Bache Halsey Stuart Metals Fund	n/a	in preparation
Comark World Metals Fund	$3,000–5000	cancelled
Goldfund	$500	in operation
Precious Metals Trust (UK)	$1.80 per sh.	in operation
South African Strategic Minerals Portfolio	$25,000	in operation
Strategic Materials Corporation	$1,250	in registration
Strategic Metals Corporation Managed Portfolio	$10,000	in operation
The Strategic Metal Trust	$10,000	in operation

In the spring of 1981, when the strategic metals investment craze took off in America, the *Wall Street Journal* and major Sunday newspapers in several cities were crammed with advertisements of strategic metals brokers. Since most of them invited you to call toll free for the latest dope on how to get on "The Gold of the 1980s" bandwagon, a large number of people responded from all over the country. More often than not they were subjected to a lot of boiler room hot air from enthusiastic salesmen playing up the greed and patriotic angles at the same time.

Much of the popular interest in strategic metals was also stirred up by the public airing of the United States' strategic minerals policies in Washington, the Soviet threat to Poland, and the United Nations' vociferous demands for sanctions against South Africa, the treasure house of strategic minerals upon which the West depends.

Despite all those factors coming to bear on the potential investors almost simultaneously and continuing inflationary pressures, only a relatively small number of prospects actually made the decision to invest in strategic metals. Money market funds were the star performers of the day. Smart guiding spirits of many an ambitious strategic metals broker operation quickly realized the need for a better investment vehicle if they planned to survive and exploit the strategic metals angle.

HOW TO INVEST IN STRATEGIC METALS

The concept of a strategic metals mutual fund, which is not unlike a commodities pool, was the obvious solution to investor resistance. This soon became clear to the strategic metals brokers, many of whom had had previous experience as gold and commodity traders. But there were a number of reasons why many of them could not proceed to implement such an idea.

Someone simply pushing metal for a living, as many strategic metals brokers do, operates in a completely unregulated market, basically as a salesman without the need to obtain any licensing from any authorities whatsoever. The capital requirements for starting a strategic metals brokerage are relatively modest. All that is needed is a boiler room with a lot of telephones and a bunch of aggressive salesmen who work strictly on commission. If they do not perform, they are simply replaced with another hungry lot, each of whom goes rapidly through his own list of prospects until his efforts yield sufficient commissions to earn him a living or he in turn disappears from the scene. Any incoming cash can be held in short-term high-interest-yielding certificates for sixty or even ninety days because "it takes that long to settle strategic metals purchases," and that float can literally help keep the business afloat until things take off and profits start flowing in.

When it comes to organizing and operating a strategic metals mutual fund or commodities pool, the startup requirements are such that many of the strategic metals brokers would not pass muster. Participation in a mutual fund involves the sale of securities and this type of investment is strictly regulated by the Securities and Exchange Commission. There are, of course, different kinds of funds, but we are talking about one that can be sold to the public through salesmen and the media.

The minimum capital requirements to start a fund are $100,000. The promoters must also file a registration statement with the Securities and Exchange Commission. Such a prospectus describes in considerable detail the fund itself, its management, the fund advisor, and all the operating procedures governing cash flow as well as the costs involved. Most importantly, the prospectus must outline precise mechanisms for redemption of the fund shares either in a public stock market or through direct arrangements with a third party funds trustee. The amount of liquidity in the proposed fund must be clearly stated and safeguards for maintaining such liquidity indicated.

HOW ABOUT A STRATEGIC METALS INVESTMENT FUND?

The registration process in the case of a new firm without a track record could take several months and the promoters would also need a clean bill of health following an investigation of their previous backgrounds by the SEC. It is doubtful that some of the strategic metals brokers could have survived such an investigation, and this is probably one good reason why many of them never even tried to form a publicly traded mutual fund.

Because the strategic metals fund or trust is a new and untried investment vehicle there are many Wall Street analysts who are skeptical about the whole concept. For the same reason the most profitable formula for the operation of a strategic metals fund has not been yet determined and will have to be tested in the marketplace. Nevertheless, the concept in general has considerable merit, if only because it goes far to provide the badly needed liquidity for strategic metals investment.

As to the promise of appreciation of capital to beat other investment vehicles, that remains to be seen. If history is anything to go by, clearly the success of such a fund will depend on quality of management and the amount of research that goes into it. The ability to obtain competent advice on international geopolitical developments affecting strategic metals trade and simultaneous high technology market developments is probably paramount in formulating buy and sell decisions in such an operation.

The investor who is interested in strategic metals has a number of choices now that require considerably less risk from the liquidity point of view. It is worth taking a look at the several strategic metals mutual fund and trust concepts that are being organized or already in operation.

Strategic Metals Managed Portfolios

This is what the strategic metals brokers hope you will buy from them, but, if properly executed in minimum trading units, you have to dish out about $250,000 for about ten of the most attractive strategic metals. If you have such cash on hand you are unlikely to need a metals broker because the metal traders will look quite kindly upon you and give you a decent deal anyway.

The question of which metals should be included in such a portfolio remains. The brokers have little or no experience in this matter, so don't bother to ask them. The metal traders may not care to give away such trade secrets. Your best bet is to fall back on the experience of Strategic Metals Corporation in London. Since June 1980 they have operated a strategic metals managed portfolio that includes between ten and fifteen strategic metals, depending on world economic conditions and political developments at any particular time. They have established a trading advisory board of seasoned metal traders who constantly evaluate up to forty industrial metals and select ten to fifteen according to a dozen or so criteria that point to the desirability of including a particular metal in the portfolio at any one time.

Unfortunately, Strategic Metals Corporation will not tell you which metals are included in their managed portfolio, which is really a highly specialized private mutual fund. The contents of that portfolio are their trade secret, but the firm also offers a ten-metal fixed portfolio as one of its services and regularly computes a strategic metals index based on those ten chosen metals.

Strategic Metals Corporation tells us that the ten metals that make up the strategic metals index have been selected in an analysis of eighty different metals and represent over 80 percent of total annual production of all the free market strategic metals. The metals of the index are chromium, cobalt, columbium, indium, magnesium, molybdenum, rhodium, silicon, tantalum, and tungsten.

The strategic metals managed portfolio of SMC is the first professionally managed strategic metals fund and was specifically designed to bridge the gap between the investor and the metals markets. Because Strategic Metals Corporation is run by a group of professional metal traders with long experience in servicing industrial metal consumers, their approach is probably more indicative of what a strategic metals fund should look like and what can be expected of it.

The report of SMC for their first year of operation of the strategic metals managed portfolio indicates that the actual increase in value of the fund was 33.4 percent, of which 9 percent went to pay the cost of storage, insurance, and administration of the portfolio. The participants saw their assets appreciate by 24.4 percent during the year. This is not bad, considering that the strategic metals index of the ten metals computed for minimum quantities for July

HOW ABOUT A STRATEGIC METALS INVESTMENT FUND?

1980 and July 1981 actually shows a decrease of about 13 percent during that period.

We do not know in what proportions and which metals were held for how long in the SMC managed portfolio, which is believed to be worth between $10 to $20 million, but the managers must be doing something right because generally the prices of most metals fell during that period.

It is almost certain that the SMC managed portfolio may contain some basic metals, such as copper, tin, lead, zinc, aluminum, and nickel, as well as precious metals like gold, platinum, and palladium that provide more flexible opportunities through futures trading at the London Metals Exchange and the New York Commodities Exchange and New York Mercantile Exchange. Not all the metals are in the portfolio at all times, of course, and in mid-1981 only fourteen metals were included. This portfolio was apparently biased toward the high technology electronics strategic metals such as germanium. There is also some speculation that the 33.4 percent appreciation of the fund was probably achieved by keeping a large portion of the assets in the form of interest-bearing short-term securities. With several million dollars of capital and very high interest rates prevailing during that period, this would have been quite possible. But if that was the case, then the portfolio was more of a money market fund than a proper strategic metals fund.

Nevertheless, the details of this particular strategic metals fund are important because it is the first one and run by professionals from the metal trading community. It provides useful insights to investors in individual metals or those who plan to start a strategic metals fund of their own, with some indications of what can be expected from such an investment vehicle and what the requirements are to run it.

The SMC managed portfolio managers point out that the two most important decions to be made are *which* metal ought to be purchased and *when* it should be sold. This can only be accomplished by constant study of the supply and demand situations performed by a competent research staff, and SMC allocates 10 percent of the profits toward its research budget. If the fund is in the order of at least $10 million, this would amount to about $300,000 per year for that purpose.

Another important point made by the SMC management is that in order to obtain the best possible price a single metal trade ought to be at least several hundred thousand dollars if an investor wants to participate on an equal footing with the professional metal traders.

From the investor's point of view, the SMC managed portfolio allows him to participate in all the metals included in the fund, though he may not know precisely which they are and in what proportions they exist in the portfolio. The minimum purchase is $10,000, but all the investors own the same metals at the same time. The SMC managed portfolio does not offer as liquid an investment as a mutual fund, however. The minimum initial period is six months, after which the client may withdraw his assets at any time on thirty days' notice.

The cost of participation in the SMC managed portfolio program includes an account opening fee of 8 percent for the minimum investment of $10,000, decreasing gradually to 1 percent for over $1 million. Buy and sell transaction and brokerage fees are additional, ranging from 2.5 percent for the minimum and .5 percent for the maximum investment.

If a client invested a minimum $10,000 during the first twelve months, he would redeem about $10,908 after paying all the fees and cashing in his chips at the end of the year, yielding him a little over 9 percent on his original investment. The guy with a million would come ahead by about 12.5 percent, due to lower fees. It seems that both could have done better by just putting their money in treasury bills during the 1980–81 period, but times will change and interest rates may go down while metal prices could escalate. Obviously this investment vehicle is for a longer time span than just one year.

The Strategic Metal Trust

This is a British offshore metals fund that has been set up in the Isle of Man in order to take advantage of its lenient tax laws. The investment strategy of this fund is more flexible than that of the Strategic Metals Corporation managed portfolio described elsewhere in this chapter. This trust invests in selected strategic metals but limits its holdings in any one metal to no more than

HOW ABOUT A STRATEGIC METALS INVESTMENT FUND?

30 percent of its assets at any given time. The trust also reserves the right to invest in shares of corporations involved in strategic metals and proposes to hold at least 10 percent of its assets in cash at all times.

The strategic metal trust was set up in March 1981 and is more like a mutual fund than the SMC managed portfolio. The value of its units is calculated every month based on metal prices and is quoted daily in U.S. dollars in the "Offshore and Overseas Finds" section of the *Financial Times* of London.

Its technical metal advisor is the long-established metal trading firm of Leigh and Sillavan Limited, who are members of the London Metals Exchange and the Minor Metals Traders Association. The Hongkong and Shanghai Trustee Ltd. are the trustees, and Peat, Marwick, Mitchell & Co. are the auditors for the firm. It is the first strategic metals fund to come into operation with internationally recognized and well-established financial and metal trading connections.

The basic operating costs of the strategic metal trust are 2 percent per year deducted monthly plus the cost of storage, and other services that the managers estimate should not amount to more than 2.5 percent under the worst operating conditions. The technical advisor, who provides the basic research function for this fund, is an independent metal trading firm well attuned to the marketplace, which incidentally spotted in time the looming shortages and price escalation of cobalt in the late 1970s. The technical advisor is compensated with a performance fee of 15 percent of the net profits of the trust, payable annually only if the fund makes a profit.

From the investor's point of view this fund is basically designed for the wealthy individual or an institutional investor. Although the minimum investment is $10,000, the managers openly indicate their preference for investments of $50,000 or more.

The basic investment fee is 5 percent for amounts between $50,000 and $100,000, and the trust deducts an additional 3 percent for small investors below $50,000. The investment fee falls gradually to 2 percent for amounts of $500,000 or above. The spread between the bid and offered price quotations also reflects an additional transaction brokerage fee of 2.5 percent, payable on purchase of units.

HOW TO INVEST IN STRATEGIC METALS

The First Strategic Metals Fund in the United States

The first strategic metals fund in the United States filed its registration statement in June 1981 and at the time of this writing was still in registration at the Securities and Exchange Commission. The offering is expected during 1982.

It is an important fund for several reasons. It responds to two of the biggest stumbling blocks in strategic metals investment: lack of liquidity and large initial investment.

Strategic Materials Corporation is the name of the first American strategic metals fund, though the name suggests it may diversify in the future to nonmetal strategics such as natural rubber, industrial diamonds, or mica and whatever else may be in short supply and of strategic use.

The immediate objective of this closed-end fund is to assemble a portfolio of strategic metals from twenty-odd that are considered the most attractive and for which there are no futures markets. The managers also propose to trade in metals options in London in order to leverage invested funds. The fund's advisor is a subsidiary of the Sinclair Group, headed by James Sinclair, who was the first to introduce strategic metals concepts in the United States. His Strategic Metals & Critical Materials Corporation has been promoting strategic metals portfolios of $250,000 or more to American investors since late 1980.

It is interesting to note in passing here that the Strategic Metals & Critical Materials Corporation was the first to advertise its services early in 1981 in major media such as the *New York Times*. Curiously, as the momentum picked up and numerous strategic metals brokers started coming out from the woodwork, Strategic Metals & Critical Materials stopped advertising its services. It is the opinion of this author that its management recognized immediately the problem of selling strategic metals to the small investor and reoriented its strategy to servicing large institutional clients and to develop the strategic metals fund concept.

The Strategic Materials Corporation issue is being managed by E.F. Hutton, the third-largest investment banking firm in the United States. This ought to give the fund considerable credibility and instant nationwide distribution. The minimum investment is only $1,250 for shares and three-year warrants giving the owner

HOW ABOUT A STRATEGIC METALS INVESTMENT FUND?

the rights to purchase the additional shares at $12.50 each. The issuers seek to raise $50 million in capital through the sale of 4 million common shares and 2 million warrants, which makes this the most ambitious strategic metals fund to date.

In comparison with the British funds already in operation, the Strategic Materials Corporation is similar and its liquidity even superior, because once sold to the public the shares of the fund will be traded over the counter. Its performance, however, will depend on trading advice, and the fund does not have as close connections with the established metal trading community as do the British funds.

The Bache Halsey Stuart Metals Fund

Perhaps an even better test of the feasibility of a strategic metals mutual fund will come when Bache Halsey Stuart Metals Company offers its metals fund to the public.

Bache is now a subsidiary of Prudential Insurance Company, the largest insurance firm in the world, and this will provide a much larger initial sales network than brokerage offices of the underwriting company alone. In addition, the Bache Halsey Stuart Metals Company itself is a professional metals trading firm that has been in business for thirty-five years, trading in precious and nonferrous metals. As such it has the inside track in that business, is a member of the London Metals Exchange and COMEX, and has also gotten its feet wet selling strategic metals contracts and portfolios to investors in Europe as well as in the United States.

Bache now offers strategic metals individually if you want them that way. The metals traded most are: antimony, bismuth, cadmium, chromium, cobalt, germanium, indium, iridium, manganese, mercury, molybdenum, rhodium, selenium, tellurium, vanadium, and titanium.

The Bache metals fund is smaller than that of Strategic Materials Corporation and in addition it will invest in basic and precious metals. Bache managers believe this will give them more flexibility and, considering the professional metals trading expertise behind this organization, it is definitely one of the strategic metals funds to watch closely.

HOW TO INVEST IN STRATEGIC METALS

Diversified Strategic Metals Funds

Another version of the strategic metals fund idea is the closed-end limited partnership and one of those, under the name of Comark World Metals, was developed by Comark Commodities, a Newport Beach–based commodities trading firm.

The investment philosophy of this fund is even more flexible than the Bache metals fund, but it is less liquid from the investor's point of view. The fund operates with $10 million capital, of which no more than 20 percent will be invested in strategic metals. Twenty percent will be in precious metals, another 20 percent in basic metals, and the remainder will be short-term securities and cash. The management believes this composition of the fund will provide flexibility and will allow the investor to see continuing and frequent movement in the fund, giving him a psychological incentive to invest.

The minimum investment in this fund varies from $3,000 to $5,000, depending on the regulations governing investment in such funds in individual states. Redemptions are made monthly on a fifteen-day notice.

This approach is designed to exploit the potential appeal of strategic metals as an incentive to invest in the fund. However, while the concept is attractive the depressed metals prices in 1981 forced the company to delay this fund indefinitely.

South African Strategic Minerals Fund

Since South Africa is a supplier of numerous strategic minerals, metals, gold, and precious metals to most countries of the industrialized West, the concepts of a strategic minerals portfolio have not been missed in that country. Such funds also perform the function of attracting investment funds to South Africa, which is intent on maintaining a favorable climate for foreign investment.

The South African strategic minerals portfolio is similar in concept to that of Strategic Metals Corporation of London. The portfolio is supervised by a computerized technical analysis system that analyzes daily all commodities on a long- and short-term basis. Trading takes place only in strategic minerals with sufficient market activity, and funds are diversified among a good number of strategic minerals in proportional amounts. The trading is performed by brokers of the Johannesburg Stock Exchange and positions are apparently taken in special commodities as well as stocks of pertinent companies involved in production of strategic commodities.

This fund is not for the small investor. The minimum investment is $25,000 and multiples of this amount. Assets must remain in the account for a minimum of twelve months before they can be withdrawn. The investor also pays an initial fee of 2 percent to cover sales and setup costs. The portfolio manager receives 10 percent of fund-increased value on a monthly basis only if that value exceeded the previous high. A foreign investor also has the advantage of investing in South African rands, which are available at a discount of about 25 percent from the official exchange rate.

Geopolitically Oriented Mutual Funds

Another approach to strategic metals mutual fund investment is linked to the probability of political unrest in specific regions of the world. The managers of such a fund bet on the fact that unstable conditions in countries that are major suppliers of strategic metals will lead to political upheavals that may result in the curtailment of supplies of such metals. As a result, or so the theory goes, the prices of those metals will increase and alternative smaller suppliers in more stable parts of the world will experience a boom in their business.

A strategic metals fund based on such concepts invests its assets in stocks of companies that mine and produce the threatened metals outside the politically unstable areas. It also keeps a part of its assets invested in the threatened metals themselves.

Such an approach offers certain advantages from the fund management's point of view. The research required to support investment decisions is simplified by narrowing it to only a few strategic metals and their major supplier country geopolitics. By limiting the scope of research in this way the fund can afford to do a more thorough job in comparison with other funds attempting to cover geopolitical and market developments for a larger number of strategic metals and countries. On the other hand, the risk is spread over a smaller number of metals, but this may be offset by a larger number of individual company stocks representing the producers of those metals in the more secure countries.

An investment trust organized along those lines was set up in London in September 1981. Its objectives are to invest in stocks of companies producing precious metals outside South Africa as well as in precious and other metals whose supplies could be threatened by political violence or revolution in South Africa. In this case the managers of Precious Metals Trust PLC are assuming that violence may erupt in South Africa in the future, disrupting strategic metals supplies from that country, and they exploit the popular media and political developments in that area such as Namibian action or terrorism and the massive emigration of whites from Zimbabwe after independence. They also believe that gold production in South Africa will continue to decline and will fall more sharply by 1990.

Their philosophy is to avoid investment in South African gold mining shares but maintain a position in gold. At the same time they are looking at companies in Australia, Canada, and the United States that are gold and precious metals producers. This is a diversified fund with the bulk of its assets invested in corporate stocks and only 10 percent in precious and other metals. Assuming that, besides gold, the fund may hold platinum, palladium, rhodium, iridium, and possibly chromium and manganese, this means that no more than 2 percent of its assets would be invested in any particular metal.

The Precious Metals Trust PLC issued 12 million shares at 100 pence each ($1.80) which gives it an initial capitalization of about $20 million. According to initial reports 8 million of those shares have been immediately snapped up by a single company, Phillips & Drew, at issue time. Thus only 4 million shares were sold to the public at large, and this may be an indication that there is a widespread belief that the philosophy behind this type of fund is a sound one.

Diversified Gold Funds

Some idea of which way strategic metals funds may develop can be gleaned from an analysis of several diversified gold funds

Figure 17: **Gold Funds in Operation**

Anglo-American Gold Investments	Oldest and largest multibillion-dollar fund based in South Africa and not registered in the United States. Invests in gold mining and finance companies.
ASA Ltd.	South Africa–based closed-end mutual fund whose shares are traded on the New York Stock Exchange. Primarily invests in top 16 gold mining companies in South Africa.
International Investors Inc.	Largest of American-based gold mutual funds with investments in gold mining and finance firms, major international industries, short-term debt securities.
Golconda Investors	A relatively small fund includes gold bullion, about 20% of assets in South African gold mining stocks, and other minerals companies.
Lexington Goldfund	Small Canadian–originated fund investing in gold bullion and South African gold mining stocks and short-term interest-bearing securities.
Precious Metals Holdings	A diversified closed-end fund registered in the United States. Its share prices are quoted over the counter. The fund invests in securities of gold and precious metals mining firms and up to 10% in metals.
Research Capital Fund	Invests up to 70% of its assets in mining securities and offers switching privileges within the Franklin Group of funds. Lowest minimum investment of $100.

Gold Funds in Operation (continued)

Strategic Investments Fund	Focuses on best quality South African gold mines but also keeps significant assets in cash and short-term debt securities.
United Services Fund	This well-established fund invested as much as 90% of its assets in gold mining stocks and 5% in mining finance.

that have been in operation for some time, as shown in Figure 17. The assets of those funds combine gold bullion, precious metals, gold mining stocks, gold mining finance firms, and short-term securities.

At least ten such funds are in operation in North America, with combined assets under their management valued at least $600 million or more, depending on the price of gold and securities in their portfolios. In addition, a multibillion-dollar South Africa-based Anglo-American Gold Investment closed-end fund, which is the largest and oldest of the gold funds, holds a significant amount of gold mining securities. Combined gold mining securities holdings of those funds represent a significant portion of gold industry securities and have an influence on prices.

The gold mutual funds are attractive to small investors, particularly during inflationary periods when prices of gold increase. The minimum investments in these funds are also relatively low, ranging from only $100 to $1,000. Some, however, have initial investment charges or fees of about 8 percent that are of the same order as similar fees charged by strategic metals funds of all types. An important convenience to the investor is the daily quotation of the prices in major newspapers.

The gold mutual funds are only a rough prototype of what strategic metals funds can be. Dependence on several different metals will provide more diversification than gold alone. On the other hand, relatively smaller markets for strategic metals will limit strategic metals fund assets to less than those of the gold funds. There is also potential for inclusion of gold in strategic metals funds and vice versa.

HOW ABOUT A STRATEGIC METALS INVESTMENT FUND?

Private Stockpiling Funds

Another approach to strategic metals fundlike investing is the formation and participation in a stockpile of one or more specific metals that is designed for direct consumption by industry after its capital appreciation function has been performed. Large industrial consumers keep stocks of strategic metals to provide raw material inputs for production at a future date. A publicly financed stockpile, designed specifically to supply a group of companies with the needed metals, would relieve the firms from making the investment, and stockholders who finance such a stockpile would expect a better than average return on their investment resulting from price appreciation of the metal when demand increases. Some of that function has been traditionally performed by the metals trading community, but with their increasing role in the global mining and metals trade, capital requirements for financing their operations are getting strained and the opportunities for additional stockpiling investing schemes are opening up.

A privately financed buffer stockpile of that category recently came into being in Japan when a group of ferroalloys producers organized a molybdenum stockpile, clearly taking advantage of the depressed prices of that metal. A similar concept has surfaced in the United States with the emergence of Strategic Stockpile Corporation. The idea is to raise capital through a public issue of stock that would provide investor liquidity and use the proceeds to purchase about one thousand tons of ferrochrome every year on the expectation that tightening control over this industry by South Africa will send prices of ferrochrome skyrocketing in future years.

It is not inconceivable that such consumer-oriented stockpiling financed by public funds could be organized and launched by some of the large strategic metals consumers, because they are in the best position to know in advance their expected demand for specific metals. This may also lead to the acquisition by large consumers of specialized metal trading subsidiaries, which in turn could develop public stockpiling investment vehicles and professionally administer such operations.

HOW TO INVEST IN STRATEGIC METALS

The situation is not unlike the 1960s when large computer users such as Boeing and McDonnell-Douglas formed subsidiary companies around their centralized computing services. Such services were sold profitably to numerous clients outside those companies and developed into Boeing Computer Services and McDonnell-Douglas Automation, two of the most successful computer service organizations operating throughout the world.

As a result investment in some of such specialized strategic metal funds may turn out to be very profitable for its stockholders. While there is always the risk of substitution, the involvement of major end-user interest in such stockpile operations would go a long way to alleviate such fears.

Starting a Strategic Mutual Fund of Your Own

If you do not aspire to issue public stock, you can start a strategic metals mutual fund of your own. For an effective investment vehicle this requires several hundreds of thousands of dollars, but if an individual does not possess the required capital he or she can organize a strategic metals investment club among a limited number of investors, or a strategic investment company with a capitalization of no more than $300,000 or twenty-five shareholders. Such corporations require minimum regulatory licensing as long as their securities are not offered for sale to the public. Liquidity is limited to the transfer of securities between shareholders, but if a track record of performance is shown, there is always a good chance of becoming a registered mutual fund.

In a private portfolio of that type it is possible to spread the risk by diversification within the various investment vehicles that have all or part of their assets in strategic metals. As a basis for such a fund the portfolio may include at the start an equal amount of assets in strategic metals and strategic metals trusts or funds. After a year or so you will know whether your own decisions pertaining to strategic metals were as good as those of strategic metals fund advisors. This will also give you an opportunity to rate the various strategic metals funds and stick with those that gave you the best performance.

If you have 20 percent of your assets in five or ten well-chosen strategic metals and only one or two double or triple in value

HOW ABOUT A STRATEGIC METALS INVESTMENT FUND?

during a year, this will go a long way to give your own overall fund performance an edge in keeping up with inflation and other investment opportunities.

At the same time another 20 percent of your assets in the shares of one or more strategic metals mutual funds may give you another boost of a similar amount. Chances are that if you have hit on the right strategic metal for that year, so will they. If, on the other hand, you missed professional strategic metals funds managers may do much better and at least make up your losses in that part of your portfolio.

The private fund should also include securities of mining companies that are included in strategic metals mining and production. If your metals increase in price, so will the fortunes of companies mining them, and this will further accelerate the growth of your assets. After all, if you are spending time researching strategic metals and their supply and demand relationships, you will have to look into companies that produce them and you are bound to spot profitable trends sooner or later. The advantage of having part of your portfolio in such stocks is the ease of buying and selling them on established stock exchanges. This adds to the liquidity of your overall portfolio or fund.

By the same token you might consider some stocks of high technology companies that are uniquely locked into use of strategic metals and are on the threshhold of a breakthrough that may open up huge new markets. This way you can cover both ends of the strategic metals spectrum by cashing in on a sudden upsurge in demand and prices and on the rapid growth of a company with an exclusive idea or product based on that strategic metal. One potential area that comes to mind in this respect is the solar power cell market. A dozen or so companies, big and small, are developing a low-cost solar cell to compete effectively with electric power generated through oil, gas, and other fuels. It is still a tossup which strategic metal will come out on top, but it is obvious that gallium, germanium, indium, cadmium, selenium, and tellurium are all in the running.

The idea of keeping a part of your portfolio in gold funds is to hedge your position and to take advantage of the gold funds that might profitably expand into precious metals or even strategic metals. The gold funds are uniquely positioned because their companies' research is heavily concentrated on South Africa and their behavior may also give you additional confirmation of what is expected in that troubled part of the world. After all, if you are in strategic metals you have to pay a lot of attention to what goes on around the Cape of Good Hope. But do not get locked into the gold fund companies' judgment either because they have different interests to protect.

Short-term securities and cash in your fund will represent varying positions, but if the emerging strategic metals mutual funds are any indication it seems wise to keep at least 10 percent in readily available cash. You do not have to worry about redemptions as a private strategic metals fund manager, which is what the public funds are up against. But you do want a cash reserve to be able to buy a metal or a stock that you are convinced is at the takeoff point.

If you are excited about starting a strategic metals mutual fund, you should get all the details from the Securities and Exchange Commission in Washington, D.C. Registration of some form may be required if your scheme involves profit-sharing agreements and investment contracts with participants in your enterprise who will expect a profit from the significant or essential managerial efforts of others.

Government Regulations of Strategic Metals Funds

The purchase and sale of strategic metals for delivery to an investor is not subject to any regulation because technically it is just the sale of a commodity paid for in cash. This is why strategic metals brokers must request that their clients take delivery of metals purchased, as evidenced by the assumption of storage, insurance, and assay charges in addition to warehouse receipts.

The Securities and Exchange Commission has taken the position that warehouse receipts may be considered to be securities, depending on whether the receipts are being offered or sold to purchasers not with a view to their acquiring and taking possession of the metals underlying the receipts but rather for the purpose of making an investment in the receipts. What this means is that you have to be careful what you get from a broker when you buy strategic metals.

Chapter 14
Which Company Stocks Are Strategic Metals Investments?

There are not many "pure plays" around, for the simple reason that strategic metals more often than not are by-products of copper, nickel, lead, zinc, or tin. These metals are produced and traded in huge quantities in comparison with strategic metals and form the basis of operations for most large, well-established metal producing companies.

The main objective of this book is to discuss investment in physical metals. Those who do that will sooner or later wonder about investing in stocks or strategic metals companies or other firms that are likely to benefit from a strategic metals boom. This chapter is a quick survey of opportunities for such investments.

The Integrated Metal Producing Companies

From the investment point of view the large metal producers could be analyzed by major country where they are based or by major metals they produce and sell.

Looking at it from a country point of view, the large integrated metal producers that present investment opportunities exist in only a few countries. These include Australia, Canada, France, Germany, South Africa, the United Kingdom and the United States. For ease of buying and selling shares the investor is further limited to Australia, Canada, and the United States.

Given the growing tensions around the world and political instability of many Third World countries, companies with assets and properties in North America are probably the soundest investments of all. This is because the largest markets for both basic and strategic metals will continue to exist in North America. Costs of production may not be the lowest in Canada and the United States, and deposits not the most economical in comparison with those in the Third World countries, but the threat of shortages and price escalations in the future promise that North American resources will be able to compete with foreign supplies.

Perhaps this is already reflected in the number of new mines and metal-processing plants that are in various stages of construction around the world. A total of $100 billion is being invested in almost 500 projects around the world during the 1979–1984 period (see Figure 18). Of those, 139 projects are mines and plants being built in Canada and the United States. All of Africa, despite its rich resources, has only 67 projects underway, compared to 61 mining projects in Australia alone.

Investment in the big mining companies may not offer as big a promise of capital appreciation as does investment in physical metal itself. However, if political unrest and strategic metals shortages contribute to escalation of prices, companies that mine and produce such metals in North America will benefit automatically.

On the other hand, these companies are diversified in production of various metals and nonmetal minerals. Investment in shares of such companies is like investing in a fund of mineral resources, and it is worth selecting those that have strategic metal assets that may appreciate significantly in the future.

One way of evaluating what those companies are worth is to figure out how much of their resource reserves back up each share of stock. One share of AMAX INC., as shown in Figure 19, represents 12.5 tons of molybdenum ore alone, as well as some copper, tungsten, silver, lead, zinc, and other minerals.

Taking just the AMAX molybdenum reserves backing each share of stock, 12.5 tons is 25,000 pounds of ore. If we assume it contains only 50 percent of molybdenum at $8 per pound at current prices, that is $100,000 without counting all the other minerals they own. Since one share of AMAX sells for $45 there is a large margin to pay for extraction, processing, and for making a profit in many years to come.

As strategic metals get scarcer and their prices start escalating

Figure 18: **Mining Investment Activity 1979–1984**

	New mines and plants
United States & Canada	139
Central & South America	107
Africa	67
Asia	65
Australia/Oceania	61
Europe	49

in the future, you will probably see Wall Street discover new value in those large mining companies. They may even refer to them as strategic minerals stocks. The author is already aware of some research efforts among Wall Street analysts with that objective in mind. Strategic metals investors will know that in most cases strategic metals will contribute only a small percentage to those companies' profits. On the other hand, strategic metals shortages and price escalations may exert some additional psychological pressure on the prices of shares of many of those companies, particularly when large mutual funds and institutional investors get into the act.

Don't Forget the Greedy Big Oils

Ever since oil became big business, all who owned oil resources were always figuring out how to get a piece of that action. Today revolutions, nationalizations, and the OPEC cartel have slowly eroded some of the power and assets of the big oil companies.

The oil companies have not been standing still, either. They have been on the prowl for coal, uranium, and natural gas resources companies for years. One common link between those enterprises is production of energy, another link is mining. This leads the oil companies straight into the various nonferrous metals producing companies. Incidentally, mining and refining are also very energy-intensive industries. If you own energy and strategic minerals there is a lot of profitable synergy in such an arrangement. The sum of such parts may come to be worth much more than the value of all these assets counted individually.

Figure 19: **Mineral Reserves per Share of AMAX INC.**

Molybdenum	12.5 tons of ore
Phosphates	9.1 tons of ore
Iron Ore	7.4 tons of ore
Copper	3.7 tons of ore
Potash	1.2 tons of ore
Lead & Zinc	0.4 tons of ore
Silver	0.13 tons of ore
Tungsten	0.04 tons of ore
Petroleum	0.2 barrels
Natural Gas	5,315 cubic feet
Coal	53.6 tons

Source: AMAX INC. Based on 62,084,114 common shares outstanding at December 1980 divided into the relevant reserve data for each mineral.

You will find that oil companies already operate strategic minerals subsidiaries such as Exxon Minerals or Chevron Resources, for example. Chances are that many of the large mining companies will become targets of takeovers by the oil firms in the future. Keep your eyes open on what the big oils are going after in the strategic metals and minerals industry. They know this game much better than you do.

Where Are Strategic Metals "Pure Plays"?

Among the stocks listed on the big board and even over the counter, there are very few companies that are 100 percent involved in the production of one or more strategic metals. Chances are that if they have been doing something right they were gobbled up by the big boys a long time ago. If not, they probably are not such a hot investment at all.

One of the recent high flyers was Oregon Metallurgical Co. (Oremet), involved in production of titanium, whose stock appreciated from $5 to over $60 per share in less than two years. ARMCO, a $6 billion steel and oil equipment company, owns 62

WHICH STOCKS ARE STRATEGIC METALS INVESTMENTS?

percent of Oremet stock and is acquiring Ladish Co., which owns another 14 percent of Oremet.

Ohio Ferro-Alloys is one of the few American ferroalloys manufacturers traded over the counter and was recently the target of an attempted takeover by a Norwegian ferroalloys production group. If the Norwegians have independent sources of chromium or manganese they know they could make a lot of money in America when the ferroalloys crunch is upon us.

The purpose here is to bring to your attention the existence of companies such as those mentioned above. A few more are identified in Figure 20. The interested reader may find more such firms by analysis of some mining and metal producer directories and portfolios of diversified natural resources mutual funds.

Investing in Strategic Metals Mining Ventures

Numerous mining ventures in North America present speculative opportunities for the knowledgeable investor. Once you are aware which strategic metals are likely to be in short supply in the future, investment in new firms exploring for these metals in North America makes a lot of sense. At least one British metals trust is investing in strategic and precious metals that are threatened in South Africa and in mining firms that produce the same threatened metals in North America. This seems like a reasonable approach to selection of stocks in the strategic metals investment game.

There are numerous penny stocks traded on several regional exchanges that offer interesting if volatile investment opportunities. Many more are traded on Canadian stock exchanges in Toronto, Montreal, and Vancouver, and are worth exploring. The Canadian weekly *Northern Miner* carriers extensive listings and prices of Canadian mining stocks as well as many company reports. You can find more details about this newspaper in Chapter 15.

The Vancouver Stock Exchange has become a leading venture capital exchange in North America for mining companies, big or small. It claims to rank second to the New York Stock Exchange in total volume traded and set a record in November 1980. Al-

Figure 20: **Some Examples of Strategic Metals "Pure Plays"**

Company name		Strategic metals assets
Alleghany International	NYSE	Owns 50% largest titanium producer
Cabot Corporation	NYSE	Cobalt, beryllium, chromium trade
Consolidated Durham	TSE	Antimony
Eagle-Picher	NYSE	Germanium, only U.S. producer
Hemisphere Developments	VSE	Columbium, tantalum, lithium
Nord Resources	OTC	Titanium, chromium, cobalt
Johns-Manville	NYSE	Platinum and palladium resources
Ohio Ferro-Alloys	OTC	US ferroalloys producer
Oregon Metallurgical	OTC	Titanium manufacturer
Teck Corporation	TSE	Columbium, gold, silver, zinc
Teledyne Corporation	NYSE	Zirconium, tungsten, columbium, molybdenum
U.S. Antimony	OTC	Antimony, cadmium, tungsten

Exchanges: NYSE = New York Stock Exchange; TSE = Toronto Stock Exchange; VSE = Vancouver Stock Exchange; OTC = over-the-counter stock

though in value of stocks it is behind the Toronto Stock Exchange, it accounted for 52 percent of all volume traded in Canada in May 1981. The secret to this performance lies in the fact that the average price of a share at Vancouver Stock Exchange was $2.80.

South African Mining Stocks

Gold mining stocks and several platinum-producing firms in South Africa have been the favorites of some gold funds, as mentioned in Chapter 13. On the assumption that strategic metals, particularly of the platinum group, will be in great demand in the future and South Africa will solve its social and political problems, these stocks look very good.

However, any deterioration of political stability in South Africa

WHICH STOCKS ARE STRATEGIC METALS INVESTMENTS?

or eruption of further hostilities with the black countries to the north will probably have a negative effect on the stocks while boosting the prices of the metals involved. Platinum and palladium, in particular, can be traded with less risk in New York commodity futures markets and on margin. Other platinum group metals such as rhodium and iridium can be purchased from metal traders and brokers and are readily portable. In comparison with investments in South African stocks, which also involve currency exchange and possible unfavorable taxation, direct investment in those metals appears to be more advantageous.

It Is Management and Not the Metal That Counts

Investing in stocks rather than pure metal may be more liquid, but the investor must now make such decisions based on the assessment of the management of the company. The fact that a company may be mining and producing a strategic metal for which demand is growing and prices are increasing does not in itself guarantee that its stock will appreciate in value.

Company profitability will determine the price of its shares, and if management is incompetent or makes incorrect decisions it may well find itself with an unprofitable operation on its hands.

The investor holding hard metal is not burdened with a need to investigate factors other than the demand and supply of the metal under developing geopolitical conditions. This same research is necessary before identifying the companies involved in production of these metals with the added requirements to try to predict their profitability. Therefore, direct investment in strategic metals, although less liquid in itself, may prove to be simpler and more profitable in the long run.

Part 4
Where to Get More Information on Strategic Metals

chapter 15
Sources

Despite repeated complaints to the contrary, there is a wealth of information about strategic metals. Unfortunately it is greatly diffused, not explicitly available, and has to be located in sources dealing with many other industries. This chapter identifies all the most useful and authoritative sources of such information and classifies them according to their specific point of view with regard to strategic metals production, trade, and consumption. The following categories of strategic metals information sources are discussed:

Governments	United States government sources
	International government sources
Metals and mining industry sources	Strategic metals producers associations
	Metal trade organizations
	Professional metals societies
	Conferences, seminars, symposia
	Corporate public relations
	Metals recycling organizations
Metals and mining publications	Metal industry statistics and directories
	Independent research organizations
	Metal industry publications
	Mining industry publications
	Books on strategic metals

SOURCES

End-User industry publications	Business, financial, and trade publications Geopolitical publications Military publications High technology industries publications

The strategic metals investor is not likely to have either the time or the background to consult or monitor all these sources of information. Indeed, there is no need to do so because there is considerable overlap and republication going on. But by knowing all the available sources of information, an investor can make the best choice of sources that meet his objectives. Alternatively, if you are using strategic metals consultants or investment advisors, familiarity with the various information sources gives you an opportunity to check them out and assess their capabilities with relatively little effort. So take your pick and pick the metal that takes your fancy.

United States Government Sources

BUREAU OF MINES, DEPARTMENT OF THE INTERIOR
4800 Forbes Avenue, Pittsburgh, PA 15213
Numerous publications of the Bureau of Mines contain detailed economic, statistical, and technological data on many strategic metals. The most useful of those are:

Mineral Industry Surveys—periodic on specific metals

Mineral Commodity Profiles—every few years on selected metals

Mineral Commodity Summaries—annual summary of eighty-nine minerals

Minerals Facts and Problems—reprints on specific metals

Minerals Yearbooks—reprints on metals and countries

New Publications—announcements of availability

CENTRAL INTELLIGENCE AGENCY
Director of Public Affairs
Washington, DC 20505

HOW TO INVEST IN STRATEGIC METALS

Some publications of the agency contain production, trade, and import dependence data on several strategic metals, particularly for countries of the Soviet bloc, Cuba, and China. Most useful of CIA publications for the strategic metals analyst are the following:
Handbook of Economic Statistics—annual data on all industries
The World Factbook—summaries of data on all countries every six months
Chiefs of State and Cabinet Members of Foreign Governments

ENVIRONMENTAL PROTECTION AGENCY
401 M Street SW
Washington, DC 20460
If you are wondering what regulation may influence the mining and processing of strategic metals in the United States, this is the place to contact.

FEDERAL EMERGENCY MANAGEMENT AGENCY
Washington, DC 20472
This organization publishes reports to the Congress of the United States on the status of the National Strategic Defense Stockpile goals, inventories, plans for disposals and acquisitions, and cost of operation of the program.

FOREIGN BROADCAST INFORMATION SERVICE (FBIS)
National Technical Information Service (NTIS)
5285 Port Royal Rd.
Springfield, VA 22161
Foreign broadcasts are monitored daily by expert analysts of the National Security Agency and are translated and published by FBIS and may be purchased from NTIS. These cover political, social, and technical developments in all parts of the world and are particularly useful for advance notice of events in Third World countries that might lead to a strategic minerals crisis. For the professionals this is a gold mine of information that the big newspapers may not get to use for weeks, months, or ever.

JOINT CHIEFS OF STAFF
Department of Defense
The Pentagon
Washington, DC 20301

SOURCES

Publishes an annual U.S. Military Posture document that provides useful and authoritative indications of defense expenditure trends in American, Soviet, Chinese, and some other armed forces. Valuable to the sophisticated strategic metals analyst who knows what he is looking for.

LIBRARY OF CONGRESS
10 First Street SE
Washington, DC 20540
This library contains one of the largest collections of documents and periodicals from all over the world. Most useful to the strategic metals analyst, however, are the various Joint Economic Committee studies and other background studies performed by the library staff for various congressional committees. Refer to the Federal Register to find out which studies that pertain to strategic metals or import dependence are in progress. Most are available from the Government Printing Office (GPO) at a nominal fee or can be inspected in major regional libraries.

OCCUPATIONAL SAFETY AND HEALTH ADMINISTRATION (OSHA)
Department of Labor
200 Constitution Avenue NW
Washington, DC 20210
Many metals are highly toxic and their uses are often under scrutiny that sometimes leads to banning or severe health protection measures, which in turn make their use uneconomic. OSHA knows which strategic metals are the most critical and why.

OFFICE OF TECHNOLOGY ASSESSMENT
800 Pennsylvania Avenue SE
Washington, DC 20510
Deals with energy, materials, and international security questions and provides congressional committees with special studies or assessments of consequences of various policy choices affecting technology applications. Always worth checking to find out what they are looking at.

U.S. DEPARTMENT OF COMMERCE
14th Street between Constitution Avenue and F Street NW
Washington, DC 20230

Publishes a wealth of information about foreign trade that can be used to monitor strategic metals import dependence on a monthly basis. FT 135 US General Imports Schedule A is particularly detailed in individual commodities and exporting countries. Don't forget the export controls and their potential effect on strategic metals trade in an emergency.

U.S. DEPARTMENT OF STATE
2201 C Street NW
Washington, DC 20520

Country desks could be useful for checking on latest developments in countries that supply strategic minerals or metals of interest to you. The Department of State also publishes individual country briefs on a continuous basis and an annual called *Treaties in Force* that could be particularly helpful when checking on country groupings that might be thinking about joint strategic metals price action or a commodity cartel activity.

U.S. DEPARTMENT OF THE TREASURY
Fifteenth Street and Pennsylvania Avenue NW
Washington, DC 20220

This is the department running the U.S. Customs Service. For those who want to check into the tariffs on strategic metals and whether it is worth importing them into the United States for investment purposes, U.S. Customs can tell all about free trade zones, bonded warehouses, and import procedures.

International Government Sources

Most countries maintain government organizations that compile and publish production and trade statistics on the output of all minerals within their control. Frequency, quality, and reliability of data vary widely, but more often than not these are the original data that find their way to many U.S. Bureau of Mines and other trade publications. If you are really serious about strategic metals you may as well get it directly from those countries, which will give you an advantage over all the others who are waiting for the Bureau of Mines to collect and republish the same data, usually months if not even years later. After all, the professional mining and trading firms are doing just that, which is why

SOURCES

they have an edge over everyone else. This section identifies such sources in countries that are important producers of strategic metals either in ore or metal form.

ALBANIAN MINISTRY OF INDUSTRY AND MINES
Directorate of Mines
Tirana
People's Socialist Republic of Albania

As a major chromite producer, Albania is of importance in the global chromium supply circuit, but as a closed totalitarian and the first officially atheistic society in the world it is extremely difficult to get any information from this country. The Albanian Chamber of Commerce publishes a monthly Albanian foreign trade magazine. Albania has no diplomatic relations with the United States, Canada, the United Kingdom, or the Soviet Union for that matter, but it is interesting to note that its government rushed to establish relations with the newly independent Zimbabwe (the fourth-largest chromite producer in the world). The Albanian Mission to the United Nations is another point of contact at 250 East 87th St, New York, NY 10028. Telephone: (212) 722-1831.

AUSTRALIAN BUREAU OF MINERAL RESOURCES (BMR)
P.O. Box 378
Canberra, ACT 2601
Australia
Telephone: (062) 499 620

Several periodicals are available from this organization dealing with the production, prices, and exports of all minerals produced in Australia, which include titanium ores, tantalite, cobalt, and many others. The major publications worth looking at are:
Monthly Bulletin of Metal and Mineral Prices
Australian Mineral Industry Quarterly
Mineral Exploration, Australia (quarterly)
Mineral Production, Australia (annual statistical book)

MINISTERIO DE MINERIA Y METALLURGIA, CENTRO DE DOCUMENTACION
Avenida 16 de Julio 1769
La Paz
Bolivia

HOW TO INVEST IN STRATEGIC METALS

As a major producer of antimony, tin, and tungsten, Bolivia is an important factor in the supply patterns of those metals. The center compiles periodic statistics on the output levels and export of those strategic and other basic metals from Bolivian mines.

INFORMATION SYSTEMS DIVISION, MINERALS POLICY SECTOR
Energy, Mines, and Resources Canada
Ottawa, Ontario
Canada K1A OE4
Telephone: (613) 995-9466 (J. F. Brennan)
This organization publishes fifty-three reviews of individual minerals produced or consumed in Canada. Strategic metals covered include antimony, cadmium, cobalt, chromium, indium, magnesium, manganese, mercury, molybdenum, platinum metals, rare earths, rhenium, selenium, silicon, tellurium, tin, and tungsten.

COMISION CHILENA DEL COBRE, DIRECCION COMERCIAL
Agustinas 1161-4^0 piso
Casilla 9493
Santiago, Chile
This organization publishes monthly statistics on copper production that also include molybdenum output and export volumes. The publication also includes prices of copper, gold, platinum, tin, and other basic metals.

MINISTRY OF METALLURGICAL INDUSTRY
46 Zhusi Street
Beijing
People's Republic of China
This ministry is the central Chinese organization supervising all mining and metal processing activities. It includes a nonferrous metallurgy department under the direction of Sun Hongru. Chances of getting something from them are pretty slim but you never know with the Chinese.

MINISTERIO DE LA INDUSTRIA MINERIA Y GEOLOGIA (MINMIG)
Havana
Cuba

SOURCES

This ministry was combined recently with the Ministry of Chemical Industry to form a new Ministry of Basic Industry. There is a Centro de Investigaciones Metallurgicas (CIME) but unless you are a card-carrying party member they are unlikely to talk to you. But you never know who has some communist friends in good standing, so let's not lose hope.

MINEMET—SERVICE ETUDES ET STATISTIQUES
Tour Maine-Montparnasse, 33 Av. du Maine
75755 Paris Cedex 15
France

Compiles and publishes monthly statistics for metals trade in France and an annual production and consumption yearbook that includes data for antimony, cadmium, cobalt, mercury, magnesium, gold, silver, tin, and uranium. One of the best and most comprehensive publications on metals in Europe.

MINISTERE DE L'INDUSTRIE, STATISTIQUES DE L'INDUSTRIE MINERALE
GEDIM
19, rue du Grand Moulin
42029 Saint Etienne
France

Annual statistics of this ministry include data on production in France of strategic metals and ores such as antimony, arsenic, bismuth, cadmium, cobalt, magnesium, manganese, gold, silver, silicon, and uranium.

INSTITUT NATIONALE DE LA STATISTIQUE ET DES ETUDES ECONOMIQUES
18 Boulevard A. Pinard
75675 Paris Cedex 14
France

The statistical yearbook of France published by this institute contains a whole chapter on strategic metals production and trade. Includes data on antimony, chromium, cobalt, manganese, molybdenum, columbium, tantalum, vanadium, titanium, zirconium, tin, tungsten, and uranium.

HOW TO INVEST IN STRATEGIC METALS

METALLGESELLSCHAFT AG
Reuterweg 14, P.O. Box 3724
6000 Frankfurt am Main
West Germany
This government-sponsored private organization publishes statistics for all nonferrous metals on a global basis including data on antimony, cadmium, magnesium, mercury, tin, and others. Long-term price histories of many metals including strategics are of some interest to chartists. Average prices and interesting price graphs are also useful.

BUREAU OF MINES AND GEO-SCIENCES, MINISTRY OF NATURAL RESOURCES
Pedro Gil St., Ermita
1595 Manila
Philippines
Telephones: 59-31-36, 59-38-91
Publishes semi-annual *Minerals News Service* report that includes production estimates of cobalt, molybdenum, chromite, manganese, gold, and silver and a surprisingly comprehensive annual report on the industry.

DEPARTMENT OF MINES, MINISTRY OF MINERALS AND ENERGY AFFAIRS
Government Printer, Bosman St.
Private Bag X85
Pretoria 0001
South Africa
Publishes comprehensive quarterly reports on minerals production and exports including antimony, beryllium, cadmium, lithium, manganese, tantalite/columbite, tin, titanium, tungsten, vanadium, and zirconium. Also contains data for gold and silver but not platinum metals.

MINERALS BUREAU, DEPARTMENT OF MINES
60 Juta St.
Private Bag X4
Braamfontein 2017
Johannesburg
South Africa

SOURCES

Issues periodic directories on nonferrous mines operating in South Africa and other periodicals and yearbooks with considerable details.

PUBLICATIONS DIVISION, SOUTH AFRICAN DEPARTMENT OF INFORMATION
Private Bag X152
Pretoria 0001
South Africa

This organization publishes the *South African Official Yearbook,* which contains an excellent chapter on mining and minerals in South Africa including production, reserves, and export data. This compilation also includes platinum group metals and uranium statistics.

GEOLOGICAL SURVEY
New Museum Boulevard
233 Visage St.,
Private Bag X112
Pretoria 0001
South Africa

This organization produces a very large selection of reports, maps, bulletins, handbooks, and yearbooks pertaining to the minerals potential of South Africa and Namibia. Not for the simple-minded, but because South Africa is such a storehouse of strategic minerals there may be indications in such data of potential discoveries and deposits of strategic metals that have a very significant effect on global supplies.

CENTRAL STATISTICAL ADMINISTRATION
Ulitsa Kirova 39
Moscow 103450
Soviet Union

This state statistical organization publishes a statistical yearbook entitled *Narodnoye Hozyaistvo SSSR* that contains production data for iron and steel and various products but not strategic metals. It is nevertheless useful in deriving certain consumption data from production levels of other products that use strategic metals. You must read Russian.

171

HOW TO INVEST IN STRATEGIC METALS

MINISTRY OF NON-FERROUS METALLURGY
Prospekt Kalinina 27
Korpus 3
Moscow 121019
Soviet Union

Contains several administrations dealing with production of gold, rare metals, titanium, magnesium, tungsten, molybdenum, mercury, antimony, tin, and other basic metals. Not known to publish anything for public consumption, since data about strategic metals in the Soviet Union is considered a state secret. You are not likely to get much from them, but you can impress other strategic metals experts with the information you know about this important ministry that clearly controls a very large segment of global strategic metals production.

BANQUE DU ZAIRE, DEPARTMENT DES ETUDES
Blvd. Col. Tshatshi
Kinshassa, B.P. 2.697
Zaire

This bank appears to act as a central statistical office in this country and prepares annual production statistics on the output of copper, cobalt, cadmium, silver, manganese, gold, tungsten, columbite/tantalite, germanium, and other metals. Its report also includes a mining production index for Zaire. You must read French for this one.

Strategic Metals Producers' Associations

There are many organizations promoting the use of one or more specific metals that are important and primary sources of information on specific strategic metals. Any unusual developments in metal prices or markets are closely watched by those groups but it must be understood that they represent the interests of metals and minerals producers and not those of the end-users. As a result data available from those sources may be biased in favor of continued use of their metals and they often act to counteract any end-user attempts to substitute costly and scarce metals by other materials.

Producers' associations are vitally interested in forecasting the demand for the particular metals and try to provide the producers

SOURCES

with basic data to decide on investment in exploration, production, or stockpiling of strategic metals. Some of these organizations are considered to be quasi-cartels and are sometimes held responsible for production controls that in turn influence the prices of strategic metals.

BISMUTH INSTITUTE
Rue Brederode 9
Brussels 1000
Belgium

CADMIUM COUNCIL
292 Madison Avenue
New York, NY 10017

CHAMBER OF MINES OF SOUTH AFRICA
5, Hollard Street
Johannesburg
South Africa

COBALT DEVELOPMENT INSTITUTE
London or Brussels—Formed in June 1981; location not decided

COBALT INFORMATION CENTER
7 Rolls Building, Fetter Lane
London EC4A 1JA
United Kingdom

COPPER DEVELOPMENT ASSOCIATION
Chrysler Building, 405 Lexington Avenue
New York, NY 10017

FERROALLOYS ASSOCIATION
1612 K Street NW
Washington, DC 20006

FERROALLOYS PRODUCERS ASSOCIATION
P.O. Box 1338
Johannesburg
South Africa

HOW TO INVEST IN STRATEGIC METALS

THE GOLD INSTITUTE
Suite 1140, 1001 Connecticut Avenue NW
Washington, DC 20036

INTERNATIONAL MAGNESIUM ASSOCIATION
1406 Third National Building
Dayton, OH 45402

INTERNATIONAL PRECIOUS METALS INSTITUTE (IPMI)
Polytechnic Institute of New York, 333 Jay Street
Brooklyn, NY 11201

JAPAN TITANIUM ASSOCIATION
Konwa Kaikan Building, 12-22, 1-chome
Tsukiji, Chuo-ku
Tokyo
Japan

THE MANGANESE CENTER
17, rue Hoche
75008 Paris
France

METAL POWDER INDUSTRIES ASSOCIATION
P.O. Box 2054
Princeton, NJ 08540

MINERAL SANDS PRODUCERS ASSOCIATION (titanium ores and zircon)
London Assurance House, 20 Bridge Street
Sydney, NSW 2000
Australia

NON-FERROUS METALS INFORMATION CENTER
Boulevard de Berlaimont 12
1000 Brussels
Belgium

SOURCES

NON-FERROUS METALS INDUSTRIES ASSOCIATION OF SOUTH AFRICA
Metal Industries House, Marshall & Simmonds St.
Johannesburg 2001
South Africa

PRIMARY TUNGSTEN ASSOCIATION
c/o Peat Marwick & Mitchell, 1 Ruddle Dol
London EC4
United Kingdom

THE REFRACTORIES INSTITUTE
1102 One Oliver Plaza
Pittsburgh, PA 15222

SELENIUM-TELLURIUM DEVELOPMENT ASSOCIATION
P.O. Box 3069
Darien, CT 06820

THE SILVER INSTITUTE
1001 Connecticut Avenue NW
Washington, DC 20036

TANTALUM PRODUCERS ASSOCIATION
1230 Keith Building
Cleveland, OH 44115

TANTALUM PRODUCERS INTERNATIONAL STUDY CENTER
Rue aux Laines
1000 Brussels
Belgium

URANIUM INSTITUTE
c/o New Zealand House
London
United Kingdom

THE ZINC INSTITUTE (also Lead Industries Association)
292 Madison Avenue
New York, NY 10017

HOW TO INVEST IN STRATEGIC METALS
Metal Trade Organizations

These range from free market metals exchanges to producer quasi-cartels or price stabilization schemes, to state-controlled metal trading monopolies as in all Soviet bloc and some Third World countries. Some major metals trade organizations identified in this section are primarily chosen because of their potential significance to worldwide metals trade. Most deal primarily with basic metals because these represent the bulk of all trading volume, but since strategic metals are also by-products of these metals, changes in basic metals trade patterns and actions of the metal trade organizations rapidly affect the availability and prices of many strategic metals.

ALMAZJUVELIREKSPORT (Soviet precious metals and powders trade monopoly)
Prospect Kalinina 29
129019 Moscow
USSR

AMERICAN METAL IMPORTERS ASSOCIATION
P.O. Box 380
Merrick, NY 11566

CHAMBRE SYNDICALE DU COMMERCE INTERNATIONALE DES METAUX ET MINERAIS
31, Avenue Pierre-ler-de-Serbie
75784 Paris Cedex 16
France

CHINA NATIONAL METALS AND MINERALS IMPORT AND EXPORT CORPORATION (MINMETALS)
Erligou, Xinjiao
Beijing
People's Republic of China

COMMODITY EXCHANGE, INC. (COMEX)
Four World Trade Center
New York, NY 10048

SOURCES

CUBANIQUEL (Cuban metals trade monopoly)
Calle 23, No 55, Vedado
Havana
Cuba

HONG KONG METALS MERCHANTS ASSOCIATION
128 Fa Yuen Street
Kowloon
Hong Kong

INTERGOVERNMENTAL COUNCIL OF COPPER EXPORTING COUNTRIES (CIPEC)
177, Avenue du Roule
92200 Neuilly-sur-Seine
France

INTERNATIONAL TIN COUNCIL (ITC)
Haymarket House, 1 Oxendon Street
London SW1Y 4EQ
United Kingdom

LONDON METALS EXCHANGE (LME)
Whittington Avenue
London EC3
United Kingdom

THE METAL MERCHANTS ASSOCIATION
Suite 721, Rand Central
165 Jeppe Rd.
Johannesburg
South Africa

MINERALIMPEKS (Albanian metals trade monopoly)
Rue 4, Shkurti 6
Tirana
Albania

MINOR METALS TRADERS ASSOCIATION
69 Cannon Street
London EC4N 5AB
United Kingdom

HOW TO INVEST IN STRATEGIC METALS

NEW YORK MERCANTILE EXCHANGE (NYMEX)
Four World Trade Center
New York, NY 10048

RAZNOIMPORT (Soviet nonferrous metals trade monopoly)
Smolenskaya-Sennaya Ploschchad 32/34
Moscow 121200
USSR

SOZACOM (Government-controlled marketing organization)
B.P. 13998
Kinshassa
Zaire

TEKHNABEKSPORT (Soviet rare metals trade monopoly)
Smolenskaya-Sennaya Ploshchad 32/34
Moscow 121200
USSR

VERENIGING VOOR DE HANDEL IN NIEUWE NON-FERRO METALLEN
Mathenesserlaan 340
Rotterdam
Netherlands

Professional Metals Societies

Professional societies collect and disseminate the latest metals technology information for the benefit of their members who are professional metallurgists and more often than not represent the metals end-user interests. These societies are also interested in furthering the use of metals in the industry in order to maintain and increase their importance. As a result opinions and information available from these sources are more likely to be balanced and realistic than those from organizations promoting the use of a specific metal. The added advantage of professional metals societies lies in the fact that they group experts dealing with various metals who are also knowledgeable in substitutions and alterna-

SOURCES

tive solutions to the use of strategic metals that are very costly or scarce. Professional metals societies exist all over the world. Listed here are those organizations in the most important strategic metals producing and consuming countries that are likely to respond with specific information to a well-formulated request.

AMERICAN SOCIETY FOR METALS
Metals Park, OH 44073

ASSOCACAO BRASILEIRA DE METAIS
Av Paulista 2073, 15 Horsa 1
01311 Sao Paulo
Brazil

ASSOCIATION METALLURGIQUE SA
Kollerveg 32, P.O. Box 3000
Berne 6
Switzerland

ASSOCIAZIONE ITALIANA DI METALLURGIA
Piazzale R. Morandi 2
20121 Milano
Italy

THE AUSTRALASIAN SOCIETY FOR METALS
Federal HQ, 191 Royal Parade
Parkville, Victoria 3052
Australia

CANADIAN INSTITUTE OF MINING AND METALLURGY
400-1130 Sherbrooke St. W.
Montreal, Quebec H3A 2M8
Canada

CHINESE SOCIETY OF METALS
46 Wusi Dajie
Beijing
People's Republic of China

COUNCIL OF MINING AND METALLURGICAL INSTITUTIONS
44 Portland Place
London W1N 4BR
United Kingdom

INDIAN INSTITUTE OF METALS
2 Sambhunath Pandit Street
Calcutta 700020
India

INSTITUTION OF MINING AND METALLURGY
44 Portaland Place
London W1N 4BR
United Kingdom

JAPAN SOCIETY OF NEWER METALS
1-13 Shinbashi, 1-chome
Minato-ku
Tokyo 105
Japan

METALLURGICAL SOCIETY OF AIME
420 Commonwealth Drive
Warrendale, PA 15086

THE METALS SOCIETY
1 Carlton House Terrace
London SW1Y 5DB
United Kingdom

MINING AND METALLURGICAL SOCIETY OF AMERICA
230 Park Avenue
New York, NY 10017

NATIONAL INSTITUTE OF METALLURGY
200 Hans Strydom Av.
Randburg, Private Bag X3015
Randburg 62125
South Africa

SOURCES

NORWEGIAN METALLURGICAL SOCIETY
Rosenkrantzgt. 7
Oslo 1
Norway

SINDICAO NACIONAL DEL METAL
Ferraz 44
Madrid 8
Spain

SOCIETE FRANCAISE DE METALLURGIE
5, rue Paul Cezanne
75008 Paris
France

Conferences, Seminars, and Symposia

There are three types of meetings dealing with strategic metals that take place from time to time in major cities of North America and in European capitals. These are investment seminars, policy conferences, and professional meetings. Although the titles of the three types of meetings may sound alike, keep in mind that they have very different objectives, not all of which are of significance to profitable investing in strategic metals.

The investment seminar is usually a promotional affair advertised in the local media and it is normally organized by strategic metals brokers, dealers, and traders who are interested in selling you strategic metals or anything else they may also have for sale, such as stocks and bonds, gold coins, or commodities.

While these seminars may offer you an explanation of how investment in strategic metals can be made, they are more likely to stress the positive aspects of such investments, counting on the fact that few individuals have the time or the inclination to undertake their own research. These meetings are worth attending because they are relatively short and cheap and give you an opportunity to assess the psychology of the market with regard to strategic metals. They may also indicate to you which metals the traders and brokers are pushing. Chances are that most of the price appreciation in those metals has already taken place and the professionals are out to take their profits. If you follow their actions at least you will be doing as well as the leading lights in this game.

You don't have to look for those meetings. Announcements will leap at you from the pages of your evening paper or your TV screen.

The policy conferences on strategic minerals have become popular since the Reagan administration took over the White House. The objective here is to seek public and media approval and promotion of various, often controversial, issues. These may include new legislation that will open up more public lands to exploration and mining, relaxation of environmental regulations, approval of budgets for new government agencies, and changes in stockpiling policies.

These conferences are heavily attended by mining companies and manufacturers who depend on strategic materials as their products and their raw materials. Some very interesting details may surface during question and answer time, but by and large the presentations are too superficial and too political to be of much immediate value to the strategic metals investor. What these conferences do, however, is create a public awareness of some ill-defined strategic materials shortage threat. The conferences are often exploited by those who sell metals to support their arguments that prices must go up in the future.

Because this is not necessarily so, the promoters and speakers at these conferences are usually very careful not to be connected with the investment aspects of the strategic materials issues they promote. As political animals they are always aware that there is the potential for a conflict-of-interest accusation should they be considered for a political appointment in the future.

Professional meetings dealing with one or more strategic metals are probably the most informative for the serious investor or analyst. They are also the most boring, often bogging down in details of little significance except to a small group of professional purists.

Nevertheless, for the most realistic assessments of future markets, demand, substitution potential, and alternatives the professional meeting is unsurpassed and is usually also well documented in the form of papers and slide or film presentations as well as practical exhibits.

The trouble is that unless you are a metals or minerals professional you may not even hear about those meetings. But if you want to stay ahead of the pack, check with the major professional societies who organize important annual events during which strategic metals issues are often discussed in great detail and with ultimate authority. If you are looking for unbiased opinions about the future of some of those strategic metals or are trying to determine the price at which massive substitutions would take place, this is where you must develop your information sources. The major professional societies that stage such events at least once a year are discussed in a separate section of this chapter.

Corporate Public Relations

Last but certainly not least are the mining and metals processing companies whose business is the production and supply of strategic metals. Most of them conduct in-house and contract research of the markets, competition, and geopolitics affecting their strategic metals, and they all use the same sources of information discussed throughout this chapter. The companies also perform their own original research, so to speak, by being out in the field risking their own capital and reputation. Their activities therefore bear watching very closely.

Companies do not always release all the data they accumulate on strategic metals they deal with. This is true for results of exploration, resource estimation, or even inventories and price forecasts—such information is often regarded as confidential and proprietary. However, those same companies are very often the primary sources, if not the only sources, of information about new discoveries and new processes that may alter the availability and prices of strategic metals very rapidly. This is because if new developments are such that they threaten a serious price erosion of a metal, the producers are naturally reluctant to release such information to the public until current investments are recovered and profits are secure. For this reason it is important to check with the local sources of information, where it is impossible to keep things secret because of observable changes in facilities and a labor force that lives and plays outside the plants or mines.

Corporate annual reports contain a wealth of information about individual mining and metal processing plants that will assist you greatly in making your decisions. Many strategic metals producers are subsidiaries of larger corporations; this is the only way to get at the details of their work.

Metals Recycling Organizations

Industrialized countries consume large quantities of basic and strategic metals. Depending on metal and energy prices, a certain percentage of demand can be met by recycling scrap containing such metals. In times of shortages those organizations can tell you what recycling potential exists in some of the strategic metals and how this will affect their price.

AUSTRALIAN METALS RECYCLING INDUSTRY ASSOCIATION
London Assurnance House, Suite 801
20 Bridge St.
Sydney NSW
Australia

BRITISH RECLAMATION INDUSTRIES CONFEDERATION
16 High St.
Brampton, Huntingdon
Camb PE18 8TU
United Kingdom

BUREAU INTERNATIONAL DE LA RECUPERATION (BIR)
Place du Samedi 13
B 1000 Brussels
Belgium

CANADIAN ASSOCIATION OF RECYCLING INDUSTRY
Suite 1101, 5799 Yonge Street
Willowdale, Ontario M2M 3V3
Canada

FEDERATION NATIONALE DES SYNDICATS DES INDUSTRIES ET COMMERCE DE LA RECUPERATION
14, rue des Courcelles
75008 Paris
France

SOURCES

NATIONAL ASSOCIATION OF RECYCLING INDUSTRIES
330 Madison Avenue
New York, NY 10017

Metal Industry Statistics and Directories

There are several outstanding directories and statistical reference books on minerals and metals production, trade, and consumption. These merit a separate section, even though most are compiled by publishers or organizations previously described in this chapter. The following directories and yearbooks will prove to be particularly useful to the professional and amateur alike who wants to know all there is to know about strategic metals in a hurry.

ABMS Non-ferrous Metals Data Yearbook
American Bureau of Metal Statistics
420 Lexington Ave.
New York, NY 10170
This statistical yearbook includes data for five consecutive years on mine, smelter and refined production, consumption, inventories, imports, and exports. It also publishes price histories for antimony, cadmium, cobalt, gold, magnesium, molybdenum, platinum, selenium, tellurium, titanium, tin, and other basic nonferrous metals.

International Directory of Mining and Mineral Processing Operations
Engineering and Mining Journal
1221 Avenue of the Americas
New York, NY 10020
This annual directory provides addresses of mining operations, their history, types of minerals produced, capacity, and executives in all countries of the world. It also has a section on consultants, financial sources, and a cross-index by metal/mineral produced. Planned expansion and financing section are particularly useful to those who are trying to peer into the future of some strategic metals availability. An extremely comprehensive directory, it has

HOW TO INVEST IN STRATEGIC METALS

the advantage of being updated annually thanks to the large staff and publishing resources of McGraw-Hill.

Metal Bulletin Handbook
Park House, Park Terrace
Worcester Park
Surrey KT4 7HY
United Kingdom
A statistical bible of the metals industry that includes prices and production statistics as well as memoranda on tariffs and specifications for all ferrous and nonferrous metals in world trade. Strategic metals included are antimony, arsenic, beryllium, cadmium, chromium, cobalt, germanium, lithium, magnesium, manganese, mercury, molybdenum, platinum, columbium, osmium, rhodium, ruthenium, selenium, silicon, tantalum, tellurium, tungsten, uranium, vanadium, zirconium, and others. Lists all metal organizations throughout the world and is truly invaluable to the professional metals trader. By knowing what is in this handbook analysts and investors will have an idea of what the industry professionals know.

Metal Statistics Yearbook
American Metals Market
7 East 12th Street
New York, NY 10003
This is the American purchasing guide of the metals industry. It provides basic production, consumption, and price statistics for most metals including antimony, beryllium, bismuth, cadmium, chromium, cobalt, gold, magnesium, manganese, mercury, molybdenum, platinum metals, silver, tin, titanium, tungsten, uranium, vanadium, and minor metals, as well as steels and basic metals. Don't trade metals in the United States without it.

Metal Traders of the World
Metal Bulletin Books
Park House, Park Terrace
Worcester Park
Surrey KT4 7HY
United Kingdom

SOURCES

The first edition of this new nonferrous metals traders directory was published in 1981 as a result of an increase in metals trading activity in recent years and a demand for such a reference. The directory identifies about 1,200 nonferrous metals trading firms in seventy-eight different countries and spells out what strategic metals are traded by which company. It will surprise you to see that for many strategic metals there are only one or a few traders who handle them regularly. Indispensible to anyone with strategic metals trading and dealing ambitions.

Mining International Year Book (Financial Times)
Longman Group Ltd.
42 Great Portland St.
London W1N 5AH
United Kingdom

International directory of mining firms, their subsidiaries, industry organizations, financing, production levels at specific mines, and other details of interest to the investment banking community. Lists such data as minerals reserves estimated under corporate control, and shares outstanding as well as recent price action. All the gruesome details of who is doing what and to whom in the world of mining.

Non-Ferrous Metal Works of the World Metal Bulletin Group
Park House, Park Terrace
Worcester Park, Surrey KT4 7HY
United Kingdom

This is one of the most useful directories of nonferrous metals smelters, refiners, semifabricators, and ingot makers throughout the world, giving you a complete picture of the minerals processing industry and its capabilities. Arranged by country, it also has an index by metal produced within each country and by specific plants. Topnotch metals intelligence.

WORLD BUREAU OF METAL STATISTICS
41 Doughty Street
London WC1N 2LF
United Kingdom

Maintains extensive worldwide metals statistics somewhat similar to the operations of American Bureau of Metal Statistics in New York.

World Mines Register
World Mining
500 Howard Street
San Francisco, CA 94105
Alphabetic listing of major mining operations in over eighty countries of the world indicates minerals produced, mine capacity, and equipment in use. A cross-index identifies mines by ores or metals for such strategic metals as chromium, manganese, mercury, molybdenum, silver, tin, titanium, tungsten, uranium, vanadium, gold, selenium, and tellurium.

Independent Research Organizations

There are several research services that perform independent proprietary and multiclient research into strategic metals markets. These firms basically draw upon the same data on strategic metals developed by all the other sources discussed in this chapter, but they try to develop an independent assessment of the conclusions presented by metal producing and consuming industries. Corporate executive interviews and specialized questionnaires are used to elicit additional insights into specific strategic metals issues.

Proprietary studies are usually relatively expensive because their performance depends on the employment of expert consultants whose rates are about $500 per day or more. Sometimes these research firms alleviate the high cost of performing such a study by syndicating the research effort on a multiclient basis. Even then the individual cost of participation in such a study could be in the order of $15,000 to $25,000, depending on the number of clients and amount of detail and time required to complete the study. You can be sure that major minerals mining and metals producing firms maintain such research on a continuing basis both in-house and by participating in independent study programs. Individual investors in strategic metals without the resources to spend on such research are always at a considerable disadvantage in trying to beat the professionals of this industry.

SOURCES

BATELLE COLUMBUS LABORATORIES
505 King Avenue
Columbus, OH 43201
Performs research and development of strategic metals substitution and recycling methods and national security problems resulting from supply disruptions. Operates a copper data center.

CHARLES RIVER ASSOCIATES
John Hancock Tower, 200 Clarendon Street
Boston, MA 02116
Performed a series of studies for government agencies and corporate clients relating to strategic metals supplies, shortages, stockpiles, and future demand. These included tungsten, cobalt, titanium, and other minor metals.

CHASE ECONOMETRICS
555 City Line Avenue
Bala Cynwyd, PA 19104
Operates a nonferrous computerized metals forecasting service on a subscription basis since 1975. Primarily deals with basic metals but is also positioned to perform strategic and minor metals analysis.

COMMODITIES RESEARCH UNIT LTD.
33 West 54th Street
New York, NY 10019
Operates computerized data banks on nonferrous metals and some strategic metals and provides short-term outlook multiclient studies on specific metals. Primarily deals with basic metals. Services are similar to those provided by Chase Econometrics.

GEOSTRATEGICS, INC.
21st Century Research
8200 Boulevard East
North Bergen, NJ 07047
Specializes in strategic metals investment and market studies for the investment community, including strategic metals mutual funds feasibility. Publishes a monthly digest, *Strategic Metals In-*

telligence, dealing with the geopolitics, markets, technology, and trade in strategic metals.

ROSSKILL INFORMATION SERVICES
2 Clapham Road
London SW 9
United Kingdom
Provides worldwide research reports on metals and minerals including all strategic metals. These reports contain a large amount of data, including detailed statistics on imports and exports of specific strategic metals between particular supplier and consumer countries.

ARTHUR D. LITTLE, INC.
25 Acorn Park
Cambridge, MA 02140
A leading worldwide research organization performing various economic and technological assessment studies for major corporations and governments. These include some special studies on metals and minerals, including those of the Soviet Union.

STANFORD RESEARCH INSTITUTE
333 Ravenswood Avenue
Menlo Park, CA 94025
A nonprofit organization performing government and corporate research, including economic studies of metals industries, some of which is available on a multiclient basis.

Metal Industry Publications

This section identifies some of the most useful sources of information to the strategic metals investor. Metal industry periodicals are more attuned to the metal trading and consumer industries and always discuss supplies, demand, prices, and new technological developments that either replace or create new demand for strategic metals. *American Metals Market, Metal Bulletin, Metals Week,* and *Strategic Metals Intelligence* are probably the most useful publications to the strategic metals investor.

SOURCES

American Metals Market
7 East 12 Street
New York, NY 10003
This is a daily newspaper with the latest available news on all metals production, inventories, trade, and prices throughout the world. It quotes daily average prices for antimony, beryllium, bismuth, cadmium, iridium, magnesium, manganese, mercury, molybdenum, osmium, palladium, platinum, rhodium, ruthenium selenium, silicon, silver, tantalum, tellurium, tungsten, uranium, zirconium, and other basic metals. The newspaper is particularly valuable because it offers immediate analysis and explanations of metals price movements based on opinions of metals trade executives.

A special weekly edition of *Metalworking News,* an offshoot of *American Metals Market,* reports on major metal end-user market developments and makes this publication particularly valuable to the strategic metals investor. Because of its frequency and specialized editorial focus this newspaper brings you more metal news and background information faster than any other publication in the world. Its annual *Metal Statistics* yearbook is an extremely useful reference and a must for any serious metals analyst and investor.

Engineering and Metals Review
Association of Indian Engineering Industry
6 Netaji Subhas Rd.
Calcutta 700001
India
This monthly magazine includes statistics for various metal end-user industries in India and a *Weekly Bulletin* that covers metal prices in India including tin, cadmium, antimony, and bismuth. Offers unusual insights into a very little known area that may rapidly increase in significance to metal markets with the industrial development of the Third World.

Finishers Management
1800 Pickwick Avenue
Glenview, IL 60025

A controlled circulation monthly primarily for management within the metal finishing field. May occasionally give very important information into potential of some strategic metals and their markets.

Iron Age
Chilton Way
Radnor, PA 19089
This is an important weekly trade magazine that includes news on metals end-user market developments. Despite heavy concentration on iron and steel and basic metals, it carries a lot of information about nonferrous and minor metals. Quotes prices for antimony, beryllium, bismuth, cadmium, chromium, cobalt, germanium, indium, iridium, magnesium, manganese, mercury, molybdenum, palladium, platinum, rhodium, silver, thorium, titanium, vanadium, and zirconium.

Journal of Metals
Metallurgical Society of AIME
420 Commonwealth Drive
Warrendale, PA 15086
A monthly publication of the American Institute of Mining, Metallurgical and Petroleum Engineers, this magazine often publishes strategic metals study results, market forecasts, and papers considering supplies, economics, and substitution technologies. Particularly useful to a serious student of the strategic metals scene who wants to find out what is happening in the end-user research area and how it might affect prices and availability of strategic metals in the future.

Light Metal Age
693 Mission Street
San Francisco, CA 94105
A controlled circulation monthly covering latest developments in the production and fabrication of aluminum, magnesium, titanium, beryllium, and their light alloys. Not essential but worth a check when looking into these metals.

SOURCES

Materials Engineering
1111 Chester Avenue
Cleveland, OH 44114
An important monthly dealing with engineering materials including all metals. Worth watching for developments that signal metal substitution potential because of price or performance considerations. Publishes *Materials Forecast for the 80s,* another useful reference for the serious strategic metals analyst.

Metal Bulletin
45-46 Lower Marsh
London SE1 7RG
United Kingdom
This bulletin is published twice a week on Tuesdays and Fridays in London and is one of the most authoritative publications on the latest prices and developments in metals trading. Quotes prices of arsenic, beryllium, bismuth, cadmium, cerium, chromium, cobalt, columbium, germanium, indium, iridium, lithium, magnesium, manganese, mercury, molybdenum, osmium, palladium, platinum, rhenium, rhodium, ruthenium, selenium, silicon, silver, tantalum, tellurium, titanium, tungsten, uranium, vanadium, and zirconium. It carries more price quotations than any other metals periodical and is widely used by metals traders throughout the world.

The *Metal Bulletin* Group also publishes a *Metal Bulletin Monthly* and several metal trade directories. The most valuable to the strategic metals analyst and investor is the *Metals Traders of the World,* which was first published in 1981.

Metals Investor
711 W. 17th Street, G-4
Costa Mesa, CA 92627
This recent monthly newsletter specializes in discussing investment opportunities in industrial metals including basic metals such as aluminum, copper, lead, nickel, and zinc, as well as many strategic metals. Quotes prices of major metals and several strategic or minor metals from other publications. Carries excellent

investment assessment of various strategic metals in selected issues and interviews with strategic metals traders.

Metal Progress
American Society for Metals
Metals Park, OH 44073
This is a monthly publication for the members of this professional society of metallurgists that carries extremely interesting though technical reports of current research into metals applications, new uses, alloys, demand, and markets. Reports on results of independent studies into metals markets and on proceedings of specific conferences and symposia. Often discusses specific use and problems associated with many strategic metals. ASM is the sponsor of the annual *Metals Week* conference, considered to be the major metals event of the year in North America. A must for the metals analyst and investor trying to forecast the future.

Metal Traders Perspective
666 Fifth Avenue
New York, NY 10103
A newsletter discussing the latest developments and prices of basic and precious metals. Useful as an indicator of basic trends since strategic metals are by-products of copper, zinc, lead, nickel, and gold.

Metals Week
McGraw-Hill
1221 Avenue of the Americas
New York, NY 10020
A weekly newsletter targeting the industrial metals consumer, quoting daily prices for basic metals and weekly producer and dealer prices for most strategic metals. Second in number of price quotes only to *Metal Bulletin,* but has the advantages of uniform U.S. dollar prices. Quotes prices of antimony, arsenic, beryllium, bismuth, cadmium, chromium, cobalt, columbium, gallium, germanium, indium, iridium, lithium, magnesium, manganese, mercury, molybdenum, osmium, palladium, platinum, rhenium, rhodium, ruthenium, selenium, silicon, silver, tantalum, tellurium, titanium, tungsten, vanadium, and zirconium.

SOURCES

Non-Ferrous Metals
1 Wenxieng Street
Beijing
People's Republic of China
This is one of the few Chinese quarterlies on industrial subjects that are available to a foreigner. The magazine discusses mining, minerals processing, and metallurgy in China. It is in Chinese, of course, but has an index in English. Chances are that the more pertinent papers and articles have been translated by Joint Publications Research Service (JPRS) and are available from National Technical Information Service (NTIS) (see "United States Government Sources," page 148). But if you insist on looking at the real thing, you can subscribe directly by getting in touch with Guoji Shudian, P.O. Box 399, Beijing, People's Republic of China, and telling them you want publication Code Q 352.

33 Metal Producing
McGraw-Hill
1221 Avenue of the Americas
New York, NY 10020
Controlled circulation monthly, dealing with metal production technology primarily in basic metals, but may offer insights into new uses of strategic metals since it covers industry innovation programs.

Modern Metals
211 E. Chicago Avenue
Chicago, IL 60611
A monthly dealing with developments in nonferrous manufacturing and metalworking plants. Mostly covers basic metals, but useful for occassional discussions of special uses of strategic metals in these processes.

Scrap Age
6311 Gross Point Road
Niles, IL 60648
This is a monthly covering major developments in the recycling of metals, including strategic metals such as cobalt and titanium, and activities of recycling organizations in the United States.

HOW TO INVEST IN STRATEGIC METALS

Strategic Metals Intelligence
21st Century Research
8200 Boulevard East
North Bergen, NJ 07047
A monthly digest covering strategic metals investment vehicles such as mutual funds, managed portfolios, brokerage, trade, markets, geopolitics, and technology. Includes reports from western, communist, and Third World sources on differing perceptions of strategic metals questions and analysis of impact on supplies, prices, markets, and national security. Developed a strategic metals price index for most active strategic metals and also identifies publicly held corporations involved in strategic metals production and trade.

USSR Materials Science and Metallurgy
Joint Publications Research Service
1000 N. Glebe Road
Arlington, VA 22201
Translations into English of most important Soviet technical and trade publications dealing with materials and metals resources and production. One of the very few sources on Soviet metal industry developments including use of strategic metals in various high technology industries. Should not be missed by strategic metals analysts who realize the impact of Soviet metal production on global metals trade.

Mining Industry Periodicals

There are various weekly, monthly, quarterly, and annual publications that report on exploration, development, investment, mining, operations, and processing of minerals throughout the world. These are excellent sources of information on strategic minerals. However, because the greatest volume of mining investment and production concerns oil, gas, coal, iron ore, and basic metal ores, strategic metals account for only a small fraction of the total coverage. This reflects the fact that strategic metals are by-products of the production of copper, zinc, lead, gold, or platinum, and since there are no publications dealing exclusively with

SOURCES

strategic metals, those identified in this chapter are the best sources of current information aside from the companies that are actually engaged in mining and refining of those metals.

Australian Mining
47 Chippen Street
Chippendale, NSW 2008
Australia
This monthly magazine covers all mining activities in Australia and parts of Oceania. Features include company profiles, government policies, investment, production, mechanization, and commentaries on all minerals including oil and gas, coal, iron ore, basic and strategic metals. Extensive "Letters to the Editor" section offers rare insights into minerals issues in the Pacific region.

Canadian Mining Journal
Southam Business Publications Ltd.
1450 Don Mills Road
Don Mills, Ontario M3B 2X7
Canada
A controlled circulation monthly that covers all aspects of mining operations in Canada. Has an excellent annual review issue in February and capital expenditure issue in October of every year.

Coal, Gold + Base Minerals of Southern Africa
The Pithead Press (Pty) Ltd. 12th Floor, Meubelsentrum
111 Kerk Street, P.O. Box 9002
Johannesburg
South Africa
Despite its title this monthly magazine covers mining and processing of many strategic minerals in southern Africa. Features include face-to-face interviews with local mining executives, profiles of specific companies, discussions of investment and labor issues, research and development on improved mining and refining methods, and industry innovations. Carries monthly production data on antimony, chrome, manganese, tantalite/columbite, tin, titanium, and uranium minerals as well as gold, silver, diamonds, coal, and many nonmetallic minerals.

HOW TO INVEST IN STRATEGIC METALS

Engineering & Mining Journal
1221 Avenue of the Americas
New York, NY 10020
One of the best monthly magazines that includes prices for almost every strategic metal and mineral developed by *Metals Week*. Covers all aspects of mining and industry economics throughout the world, and in March every year has an excellent annual review and outlook issue prepared by authorities in trade of specific strategic and other metals. Also publishes the E&MJ International Directory of Mining and Mineral Processing Operations.

Indian Minerals
Geological Survey of India
29 Jawaharlal Nehru Road
Calcutta 700016
India
Discusses the occurrence and potential of various strategic and other minerals throughout the subcontinent of India and Southeast Asia. Unique.

Industria Mineraria
Via Sardegna 14
00187 Roma
Italy
A bimonthly covering the production of minerals in Italy and one of the few foreign language periodicals mentioned here. Primarily this is because the Italians are closer than anyone else to Albania and are more likely to report and evaluate strategic minerals development in that ignored but important country in the strategic metals world. The magazine also quotes mining stocks and prices at London Metals Exchange.

Industrial Minerals
Park House, Park Terrace
Worcester Park, Surrey KT4 7HY
United Kingdom
This monthly magazine is from the Metal Bulletin Group stable in England. It covers nonmetallic minerals, which include many ores of strategic metals. Quotes prices of antimony, chromite,

SOURCES

lithium, magnesium, and zirconium ores, but be careful to make sure what metal content these represent when using such figures.

Latin American Mining Letter
Miller Freeman Publications
500 Howard Street
San Francisco, CA 94105
A weekly newsletter in the process of being introduced by the publishers of *World Mining* monthly. Proposes to cover projects, exploration, technology, production, markets, prices, and financing of mining ventures in Latin America.

Minerals Report
951 Pershing Drive
Silver Spring, MD 20910
A biweekly newsletter discussing new plants, finds, stockpile action, labor in industry, EPA and OSHA news, and some international issues. Primarily deals with basic metal minerals but useful in keeping track of the wider mining issues in the United States.

Mining Activity Digest
1221 Avenue of the Americas
New York, NY 10020
A monthly digest from the *Engineering & Mining Journal* of McGraw-Hill establishment, this contains only mining activity news in exploration, development, mining, processing, smelting, refining, and financing of minerals industry. No advertising—of use to those who do not have the patience to go through the voluminous magazine itself.

Mining Congress Journal
1920 N Street N.W.
Washington, DC 20036
A monthly publication of the American Mining Congress, this magazine deals with mining legislation and issues pertaining to labor, safety and environmental regulation, as well as engineering aspects of the industry. Good discussions of investment in developing countries, strategic minerals issues, and their impact on national security.

HOW TO INVEST IN STRATEGIC METALS

Mining and Engineering
Thomson Publications
P.O. Box 1683
Salisbury
Zimbabwe
The value of this local monthly lies in the fact that it focuses attention on generally little-known details concerning Zimbabwe mining policies, its new industrial development programs, foreign investment regulations, and labor issues. Provides monthly production and export sales data on chrome, cobalt, gold, tin, and tungsten, as well as ferroalloys and base metals produced in Zimbabwe. Also features Zimbabwe Stock Exchange mining shares index. A must for African geopolitics watchers with regard to strategics.

Mining Journal
The Mining Journal Ltd.
15 Wilson Street
London EC2M 2TR
United Kingdom
One of the most comprehensive weekly newsletters dealing with worldwide mining activities and one of the few publications with a relatively good coverage of Latin American developments. Quotes prices of antimony, arsenic, beryllium, bismuth, cadmium, cerium, chromium, cobalt, columbium, indium, magnesium, manganese, mercury, molybdenum, osmium, palladium, platinum, rhodium, selenium, silver, tellurium, titanium, tungsten, vanadium, zirconium. This is more than an investor can handle at any one time. They also publish a monthly *Mining Magazine* and a *Mining Annual Review,* which is one of the most complete yearbooks dealing with individual metals and minerals, their markets, countries of origin, and geopolitics.

Northern Miner
7 Labatt Avenue
Toronto, Ontario M5A 3P2
Canada
This is the most comprehensive weekly dealing with Canadian mining developments in ores, oil, and gas. Also carries many

SOURCES

authoritative comments on metal markets and quotes prices of antimony, bismuth, cadmium, cobalt, magnesium, platinum, silver, tungsten, and gold. Particularly interesting because of extensive mining stocks price quotations on Toronto, Montreal, Vancouver, Alberta, and over-the-counter exchanges in Canada.

Skillings Mining Review
700 First Federal Savings Building
Duluth, MN 55802
Mainly this weekly discusses basic ores mining, but it includes prices of gold, iridium, tin, rhodium, cadmium, silver, molybdenum, bismuth, and vanadium every week. Also has some quotes of American, Canadian, and foreign stocks of companies engaged in mining and metal processing.

Western Miner
1201 Melville Street
Vancouver, BC V6E 2X9
Canada
Major interest of this monthly is western Canadian mining activity at the project level with some refining discussions. Of interest to the more sophisticated investor who is looking for special by-product potential in the mining of gold and basic minerals in the region.

World Mining
Miller Freeman Publications
500 Howard St.
San Francisco, CA 94105
Covers mining around the world with emphasis on methods and equipment. It is edited from San Francisco and Brussels simultaneously and issues a very useful *World Mining Yearbook* that covers developments in seventy-three countries.

Books on Strategic Metals

Very few books are available so far that discuss strategic metals exclusively, although many of the metals are covered in numerous technical volumes and other reference books. Actually, for the investor, only books describing methods and procedures for profitable investment are of interest because periodicals contain much more current information on strategic metals production, consumption, markets, and prices. Nevertheless there are a few books that are useful as an introduction to several aspects of strategic metals geopolitics, trade, and consumption issues, and these are reviewed briefly in this section.

Get Really Rich in the Coming Super Metals Boom (1980)
by Gordon McLendon
Simon & Schuster
New York, NY

Unfortunately this book fails to live up to its title because it turns out to be mostly a series of patriotic statements by a Texas millionaire who finally tells you that he traded some metals for his own account and made some profits. When you read about all the effort he has gone through to do it and you know he is a wealthy businessman you cannot but wonder why Mr. McLendon would even bother. Interesting nevertheless as one of the first books to mention something like indium or germanium as an investment but fails to convince you that there is a very easy path to riches through strategics.

Guide to Non-Ferrous Metals and their Markets (1979)
by Peter Robbins and John Edwards
Kogan Page Ltd.
London

This is a well-organized handbook clearly designed for the professional metals trader rather than private investor. Provides production and price history information about most basic and minor metals. (Platinum, palladium, rhodium, iridium, ruthenium, and osmium are covered in a companion book, *Guide to Precious Metals,* by the same author.) It has an appendix with a list of member firms of the Minor Metals Traders Association and the London Metals Exchange. If you have ever wondered where the strategic metals brokers get their trading contracts, this is it. If you have an ambition to become a strategic metals pusher, get the book by all means, but you can get more up-to-date production

SOURCES

and price data from many other sources previously discussed in this chapter.

How to Avoid Strategic Materials Shortages (1981)
by Bohdan O. Szuprowicz
John Wiley & Sons, Inc.
New York

This is my own effort to sort out the fundamentals of non-oil strategic minerals trade around the world. My chosen title was "Strategic Materials Geopolitics" which is what the book is all about, but my publisher, in cahoots with a national bookstore chain, decided they knew better and switched it on me. If you have ever wondered what the worst possible scenario might be, read my chapter on strategic materials supercartel, which incidentally identifies all the geopolitically most vulnerable strategic metals.

Investing in Natural Resources (1980)
by Walter Youngquist
Dow-Jones Irwin
Homewood, Il

A very readable roundup of major suppliers of all natural resources, including timber and farmland as well as oil and gas and all metal-bearing minerals. It concentrates on investment in shares of companies mining and refining metals and was obviously written before the current mania of direct metal investment.

The Mining Industry and the Developing Countries (1977)
by Rex Benson and Benison Varon
The World Bank
New York

Not for the impatient and greedy investor who is itching for action in strategics, this is a serious study of all the aspects of mining in Third World countries. It brings out some of the underlying reasons for political instability, underinvestment, and the New International Economic Order ideas. A valuable reference for the serious analyst who is looking for comparative statistics and Third World or United Nations opinions about mining investments and returns in various countries.

HOW TO INVEST IN STRATEGIC METALS

The New Scramble for Africa (1974)
by E. A. Tarabrin
Progress Publishers
Moscow

An extremely interesting book that puts forth the Soviet point of view about western exploitation of Africa. It discusses western dependence on Southern Africa's minerals several times and gets into details of various arrangements between western corporations and oppressive regimes as seen by the Russians.

South Africa's Strategic Resource (1977)
by W. C. J. van Rensburg and J. A. Pretorius
Valiant Publishers
Johannesburg

An exquisite exposition of South Africa's strategic importance as a supplier of critical minerals to the West. The discussions include comparisons of Soviet and South African dominance in certain strategic minerals and the potential Marxist threat to western minerals supplied by the High Africa region. Extensive statistical presentations make this book a valuable source of information about the minerals of the region and the South African position.

Strategy and Economics (1961)
by A. N. Lagovskyi
Soviet Ministry of Defense
Moscow

This mysterious book by a Soviet general actually exists and I have seen an old yellowed copy. It discusses western dependence on Third World sources of strategic minerals and includes the argument that a chromium denial policy could effectively paralyze the western NATO alliance and destroy western industries. Somewhat dated but interesting example of Soviet thinking with regard to strategic minerals. Unfortunately, it is available only in Russian, and you may have a job finding a copy even then because the Russians prefer to say they have never heard of the book. But if you insist on seeing and reading it there is still a copy at the Slavonic Division of the New York Central Library. Hurry up before the KGB liquidates that one too.

SOURCES

Business, Financial, and Trade Publications

Because strategic metals are becoming an important new investment vehicle, the merits of such investments are often discussed by the world's business press. Included here is a list of major financial and business periodicals that have in the past carried articles or studies of the strategic metals question in one form or another. If you have time for only one then the *Financial Times* of London is probably your best bet. It is international in scope, and London remains the world's metals trading capital.

African Business
63 Long Acre
London WC2E 9LR
United Kingdom
A monthly that claims the largest business circulation in Africa provides vary useful insights into black Africa's business and finance developments but has a heavy Third World bias.

Barron's Weekly
22 Cortland Street
New York, NY 10007
The best weekly with the most comparative financial data in the United States. If you are an investor in any other commodities you already know all about it. Carries occasional in-depth articles on strategic metals and associated investments.

Business Week
1221 Avenue of the Americas
New York, NY 10020
A leading business weekly carrying many well-researched articles on strategic metals, defense industry, other high technology end-user industries.

China Business Review
1050 17th Street NW, Suite 350
Washington, DC 20036

A unique bimonthly publication, probably the most comprehensive in the world on China trade, with very extensive reports and studies on Chinese minerals and strategic metals trade.

Financial Times
Bracken House, 10 Cannon Street
London EC4B 4BY
United Kingdom
A prestigious newspaper with worldwide coverage of financing and trade. Often carries extensive articles on various metals industries. First to quote British Strategic Metals Trust prices in its offshore trusts and funds section.

Financial Post
481 University Avenue
Toronto M5W 1A7
Ontario
Canada
A leading Canadian financial newspaper dealing with domestic and international business and trade issues.

Japan Economic Journal
1-9-5 Otemachi, Chiyoda-ku
Tokyo 100
Japan
One of the best monthly roundups of international business and trade as seen uniquely from the Japanese point of view.

Purchasing
221 Columbus Avenue
Boston, MA 02116
A biweekly magazine that often discusses strategic and critical materials issues for the benefit of the purchasing manager. Good industrial point of view and inventory potential data.

South Africa Financial Mail
Carlton Center, P.O. Box 9959
Johannesburg
South Africa

SOURCES

Among the leading financial newspapers presenting the details of South Africa's financial and trade developments. Of significance to the strategic metals investor and trader because of the major sources of strategic minerals in that country.

Soviet Foreign Trade
An official government monthly promoting Soviet exports that nevertheless provides unusual insights into the Soviet point of view on various strategic metals and their western markets. Very useful because it lets you keep an eye on what the Soviets are pushing at any one time.

Usine Nouvelle
59, rue du Rocher
75008 Paris
France
A leading French biweekly magazine, often discusses the French point of view on strategic metals and quotes prices for many in francs.

Wall Street Journal
You don't need a review of this one. You know it's worth a look every day.

Geopolitical Publications

Because political factors are becoming increasingly important in strategic metals trade it is necessary to monitor political developments in major strategic minerals supplier countries. South Africa, the Soviet Union, Australia, Canada, China, Latin America, and some Southeast Asian countries are the most important.

Major newspapers such as the *New York Times* or *Washington Post* normally report on developments throughout the world, but there are several periodicals that discuss political issues of specific regions in more detail and may often provide warning of an impending crisis before it is reported in the general media. The problem with such lesser-known publications is their credibility and the time and foreign languages often required to monitor them.

For these reasons this section lists mostly English language publications that are readily available in the West. Anyone who bothers to read some of these may be surprised at how differently strategic minerals issues are perceived by European socialists, communists, or African liberation promoters, but you must keep in mind that even though such views are unpopular in the United States and are often not even reported by American media, there are large numbers of people elsewhere in the world that believe and act upon such perceptions. If you have an open mind and are willing to accept a lot of criticism of your point of view you will find many useful indications in such literature that may help you stay ahead of your competition.

Africa
Kirman House 54a, Tottenham Court Rd.
London W1P OBT
United Kingdom
This is a business, economic, and political monthly reporting on developments in all African countries and promoting the view of the Organization of African Unity (OAU) that strongly opposes the South African policies.

Afrique-Asie (in French)
13, rue d'Uzes
75002 Paris, France
A biweekly magazine published by Third World liberation promoters who are pushing the New International Economic Order and report on the political development in African, Mideast, and Asian countries. They often provide little-known details of meetings and confrontations between western business, government, and social leaders, Soviet bureaucrats, and Third World leaders.

Africa Economic Digest
MEED Ltd.
21 John St.
London WC1N 2PB
United Kingdom
This is a companion weekly news, analysis, and forecast magazine to the Middle East Economic Digest (MEED). It contains coun-

SOURCES

try-by-country reports of the latest economic conditions throughout Africa. It includes a weekly review of main African commodities, foreign trade statistics, and currency exchange rates.

Africa Now
Pan-African Publishers Ltd.
Dilke House, Malet St.
London WC1E 7SA
United Kingdom
Another monthly roundup of the more militant African groups, also reflecting the position of the Organization of African Unity (OAU) and liberation groups with country-by-country reports and heavy correspondence from English-speaking Africa.

African Report
833 United Nations Plaza
New York, NY 10017
Published by the African-American Institute, this bimonthly magazine is designed for those with a professional and personal interest in Africa.

Americas
OAS
17th and Constitution Ave., NW
Washington, DC 20006
A monthly publication reflecting the position of the Organization of American States (OAS) of North and South America.

BBC Summary of World Broadcasts
BBC Monitoring Service
Caversham Park
Reading RGA 8TZ
United Kingdom
Daily translations of radio broadcasts from Africa, China, Southeast Asia, eastern Europe, and the Soviet Union. Carries much information about new sources of strategic minerals, investments, trade agreements, and meetings between political and business leaders not found in general press. Extremely valuable for those who are keen to stay ahead of the news.

Beijing Review
Guoji Shudian, P.O. Box 399
Beijing
People's Republic of China
Reflects Chinese position on latest developments in all countries of the world, but also carries official announcements of China's minerals output and trade. A must for those who believe China is a new, unexplored minerals frontier that may affect strategic metals supplies in the future.

Brazil Trade and Industry
Fundacao Visconte de Cabo Frio, Ministerio de Relaciones Exteriores
70170 Brasilia (DF)
Brasil
Official government trade promotion publication that carries descriptions of minerals discoveries and production and trade in Brazil. Chances are that you do not read Portuguese, so this is your best bet to get an idea of the latest on Brazil's trade and development policies.

Economist
25 St. James's Street
London SW1A 1HG
United Kingdom
One of the best weekly magazines that covers developments all over the world and provides an analysis behind the events. Often carries very well-researched articles about strategic metals and all the associated issues. A must for anyone with a little time to look at more specific sources.

Foreign Affairs
Council on Foreign Relations
58 East 68th Street
New York, NY 10021
A prestigious quarterly that publishes papers and discussions of major issues, including many that touch on strategic minerals, cartels, the New International Economic Order, and international trade.

SOURCES

Foreign Policy
11 Dupont Circle NW
Washington, DC 20036
A quarterly publication of the Carnegie Endowment for International Peace that often discusses international resources issues with regard to the foreign policy of the United States.

International Security
Harvard University
79 Boylston Street
Cambridge, MA 02138
A quarterly publication that carries extremely well-documented articles and papers on various geopolitical issues, including strategic resources and their relationship to the arms race.

Moscow News
Four Continent Books Corp.
149 Fifth Avenue
New York, NY 10010
A weekly newspaper in English that presents the Soviet point of view of the latest developments in the world. Useful if you do not know Russian and want to know what *Pravda* said the previous week.

New African
63 Long Acre
London WC2E 9LR
United Kingdom
Another monthly from England promoting the North-South dialogue and the views of the Organization of African Unity. Also publishes travellers' guides to all of Africa.

Southern Africa Forum
P.O. Box 41305, Craighall
Johannesburg 2024
South Africa
Publishes a series of position papers on all aspects of African geopolitics from the South African point of view. Also performs extensive studies on the future potential of the southern African

region; includes numerous statistics on strategic resources, production, and trade.

South Africa International
South Africa Foundation, P.O. Box 7006
Johannesburg
South Africa
or 1225 19th St. NW, Suite 620
Washington, DC 20032

This is a quarterly with scholarly articles and commentaries on South Africa's foreign policy. Registration of the South Africa Foundation as a foreign agent with the U.S. Department of State marks this organization as a propaganda agency of the South African government.

World Press Review
P.O. Box 915
Farmingdale, NY 11737

A useful monthly roundup of editorials and articles and discussions on current issues in major newspapers of the world. Provides a comparative assessment of the differing perceptions of the same events during the preceding month.

International Affairs Bulletin
South Africa Institute of International Affairs
Jan Smuts House
P.O. Box 31596
Braamfontein, 2017
Johannesburg
South Africa

A publication that explains the South African point of view on that country's foreign policy objectives.

Military Publications

Because modern weapons are often dependent on strategic metals that are irreplaceable in many such applications, the armed forces of the world are an important and growing market. Listed in this section are several leading military periodicals that discuss

SOURCES

military equipment rather than doctrine, tactics, or strategy. A familiarity with some of these relatively little-known publications will give you an ability to zero in on those strategic metals where substitution resulting from price escalation is not likely to take place.

Air Force Magazine
1750 Pennsylvania Ave., NW
Washington, DC 20006
Provides excellent assessment of military aircraft deployed by major air forces of the world and a good basis for forecasting many markets for strategic metals that you know are used in such aircraft.

Defense Week
300 National Press Bldg.
Washington, DC 20045
A weekly newsletter that focuses on American and international strategic affairs, weapons development, budgets, and government policies. Useful to keep track of military programs on a current basis.

International Defense Review
86 Ave. Louis Casai, Box 162
1216 Cointrin-Geneve
Switzerland
Monthly roundup of latest weapons systems manufactured by leading suppliers with detailed descriptions of capabilities and components.

Jane's Weapons Systems
238 City Rd.
London ECIV 2PU
United Kingdom
One of the best annual directories of weapons systems manufactured and deployed throughout the world. The publisher is also famous for its very well-known yearbooks dealing with aircraft, ships, railroads, and other weapons of the world. A must for anyone specializing in military markets.

HOW TO INVEST IN STRATEGIC METALS

Military Electronics/Countermeasures
2065 Martin Avenue, Suite 104
Santa Clara, CA 95050
This is one of the very few trade publications dedicated to electronic warfare equipment and its special requirements for strategic metals. Requires some understanding of electronics and technical lingo but is a wealth of information on the anatomy of electronic warfare.

Military Balance
International Institute for Strategic Studies
23 Tavistock St.
London WC2E 7NQ
United Kingdom
Annual assessment of world weapons inventories and defense budgets in every country of the world by an international group rumored to be financed by western intelligence services. Indispensable to those who want to keep track of where the strategic metals are used in military material.

Military Review
U.S. Army Command & General Staff College
Ft Leavenworth, KS 66027
A monthly discussing tactics and strategy and also equipment of the U.S. Army within the context of military forces of the world.

Military Technology
Postfach 140187
Bonn
West Germany
One of the best monthly magazines describing modern weapons in detail and very valuable for assessment of emerging weapons markets and strategic metals requirements. Don't study military markets without looking at this magazine first.

Nato's Fifteen Nations
Jules Perel's Pub. Co.
P.O. Box 913, 35 Matterhorn
1186 EB Amstelveen
The Netherlands

SOURCES

An excellent bimonthly that discusses not only the armed forces and equipment of NATO countries but also of their opposition, the Third World, and potential future alliances and military groupings.

Naval Forces
High Chimneys
Westwood Rd.
Windlesham, Surrey
United Kingdom
A new bimonthly on world navies and latest technologies applied to naval weapon systems at sea and in the air. Contains comprehensive documentation on current naval forces.

Soviet Military Review
2 Marshal Biruycov St.
Moscow 123298
USSR
Official Soviet government publication in English and other foreign languages describing the mission and reason for Soviet armed forces. Do not expect to find out how many kilos of germanium the Soviets need for their infrared sensors, but comparative data weapon for weapon can be derived to assess markets.

High Technology Publications

Strategic metals consumers are heavily concentrated among high technology industries such as aerospace, chemicals, electronics, nuclear power, petroleum processing, and many lesser-known areas where various metals, because of their unique properties, permit innovation to take place and productivity to increase. High technology publications are too numerous and technical in most cases, and keeping track of developments in all the different industries is a monumental task. However, there are several representative magazines for management executives in those industries that will let you keep track of the latest developments in the use and criticality of strategic metals in high technology applications. Even an occasional scanning of those periodicals will give you a significant advantage over those who simply rely on the word of a broker.

Aviation Week and Space Technology
1221 Avenue of the Americas
New York, NY 10020
Covers aircraft, rockets, missiles, space vehicles, jet engines, and avionics and related equipment. It is so good and comprehensive that even the U.S. intelligence leaders often agree that the Russians can get most of their high technology information from this magazine. An absolute must for anyone even thinking about strategic metals.

Automotive Week
965 East Jefferson Avenue
Detroit, MI 48207
If you think you know all there is to know about automobiles because you drive one, try to look at this magazine. Covers production and associated problems in an industry that is consuming masses of all types of metals including many strategic catalytic metals.

Chemical Week
1221 Avenue of the Americas
New York, NY 10020
It may come as a surprise to you, but chemicals are probably the largest consumers of strategic metals in compound forms in paints, vitamins, and just about any use. It is the mainstay of many strategic metals markets and bears watching, because in some cases new raw materials may make a strategic metal so obsolete that no one may want to produce it when the chemical market dries up, no matter how critical it may be.

Electronics
1221 Avenue of the Americas
New York, NY 10020
The leading magazine in electronics technology developments all over the world with excellent annual forecasts of electronics production and consumption in various international markets. The Russians translate it every time and print their own version for distribution to their own electronics industry.

SOURCES

Electronic Business
Cahners
221 Columbus Avenue
Boston, MA 02116
This is more palatable to the layman and business executive by announcing significant developments and discussing electronics markets and demand for various materials and equipment. Certainly worth watching, but it will surprise you how rapidly a strategic metal may come into fashion and be discarded in this industry.

Electronic News
7 East 12th Street
New York, NY 10003
A weekly newspaper keeping track of all the developments in electronics defense procurement, computers, instruments, and what the Japanese are up to. Excellent value for money in this industry if you have the time to scan it every week. Has special section on electronic materials and strategic metals used in this industry and is a sister publication of the *American Metals Market*.

Industry Week
Penton Place
1111 Chester Avenue
Cleveland, OH 44114
Excellent weekly roundup of ideas, technologies, and business decisions that affect industry as a whole. Sorts it out for you in order of importance.

Nuclear News
American Nuclear Society
555 N. Kensington Ave.
La Grange Park, Illinois 60525
Latest developments in the nuclear industry, not only in North America but all over the world. Keeps this important strategic metals consumption area in perspective.

Oil and Gas Journal
1421 S Sheridan Rd.
Tulsa, OK 74101

Covers all phases of the petroleum industry and is important because of the significance of strategic metals in catalytic processes of petroleum.

Technology Review
MIT
Cambridge, MA 02139
Discusses the latest developments in science, engineering, and related disciplines, including the effect on management and society. One of the best monthly overviews of the frontiers of technology with excellent reference materials throughout. If you only have time to look at this one magazine you will find yourself way ahead of most. This is not a boring technical magazine but a well-written periodical designed for the top industry managers and technology leaders in the world.

Index

ACLI International, 65
Aerospace industry, 70, 125
 use of composites, 47-48
 use of strategic metals, 14-15, 42, 46, 47, 92
Africa, 31, 67, 154, 155, 208, 209, 211
Albania, 34, 69, 70, 167, 177, 198
Algeria, 34
Alleghany International, 158
Aluminum, 3, 9, 29, 30, 33, 47, 59, 139
 from scrap, 50
 information sources, 192, 193
 investing in, 64, 90
 production, 33
 stockpiling, 55
 substitutes, 44, 45
AMAX Inc., 154, 156
American Bureau of Metal Statistics, 185
American Institute of Mining, Metallurgical and Petroleum Engineers, 192
American Mining Congress, 199
American Society for Metals, 194
Anglo-American Gold Investments, 147, 148
Angola, 4, 26, 69, 70, 119, 127

Antimony, 82, 85, 158
 abundance, 21
 cartel and monopoly effects, 37, 70, 122
 criticality and substitution, 43-45
 electronics and electro-optics metal, 92, 93
 from scrap, 51
 information sources, 168-70, 172, 186, 191, 192, 194, 197, 200, 201
 investing in, 92, 93, 143
 political vulnerability, 32-34, 96
 price, 73, 122-24
 production, 31-34, 37-39, 70
 stockpiling, 55
 trading units and purity level, 99
 uses, 5-9, 17
Arbitration agreements, 19
ARMCO, 156
Arsenic, 82
 abundance, 21
 by-product, 83
 criticality and substitution, 43-45
 electronics metal, 93
 from scrap, 50, 51
 information sources, 169, 186, 193, 194, 200
 investment in, 96
 price, 73
 production, 33, 39

 trading units and purity level, 99
 uses, 5, 11
ASA Ltd., 147
Asia, mining investments, 155
Assays certificate, 113, 117, 128, 132, 152
Australia, 25, 34, 36, 37, 82, 146
 information sources, 167, 179, 184, 197
 mining and metal production, 153-55
Auto emission controls, 16-17

Bache Halsey Stuart Metals Company, 65, 102
 Metals Fund, 135, 143
Basic metals, 3, 21, 22, 30, 144
Bauxite, 30, 31, 36, 55
Belgium, 77, 127, 184
Beryllium, 158
 abundance, 21
 criticality and substitution, 43-45
 from scrap, 50, 51
 information sources, 170, 186, 191-94, 200
 investment in, 96
 political vulnerability, 33, 34
 price, 73, 123, 124
 production, 30, 33, 34, 39
 stockpiling, 55

219

INDEX

Beryllium (*continued*)
  toxicity, 84, 96
  trading units and purity level, 99
  uses, 6, 8, 13
Bismuth, 33, 82
  abundance, 21
  from scrap, 50, 51
  information sources, 169, 173, 186, 191–94, 200, 201
  investing in, 143
  price, 73, 123, 124
  production, 39
  stockpiling, 55
  substitutes, 44, 45
  trading units and purity level, 99
  uses, 8, 17
Bismuth Institute, 173
Boeing Computer Services, 150
Bolivia, 34, 36, 37, 122, 167–68
Brazil, 29, 34, 38, 179, 210
Broker; *See* Commodity broker; Metals broker
Buffer stocks, 36, 38, 56, 68, 149
Bulgaria, 69
Burma, 36
By-product dependence, 96–97

Cabot Corporation, 158
Cadmium, 33, 82, 93, 158
  abundance, 21
  by-product, 37, 83
  criticality and substitution, 43–45
  from scrap, 51
  information sources, 168–73, 186, 191–94, 200, 201
  investing in, 143
  political vulnerability, 33, 34
  price, 23, 73, 123, 124
  production, 23, 33, 34, 39
  stockpiling, 55
  toxicity, 84, 96
  trading units and purity level, 99
  uses, 5, 11, 13, 17, 151
Cadmium Council, 173
Canada, 25, 146
  gold fund, 147

information sources, 168, 179, 184, 197, 200–01, 206
investment laws, 81–82
mining and metal production, 153–55
stock exchanges, 157–58
strategic metals, 29, 34, 37, 82
Cartels, 35–38, 56, 122
  investment consideration, 96
  state controlled, 67–70
Catalytic metals, 16, 17
  investing in, 92, 94, 101, 118
  metals included, 93
Central Intelligence Agency (CIA), 163–64
Ceramics, 46–48
Cerium, 200
Cesium, 17, 33, 193
  abundance, 21
  from scrap, 51
  production, 30, 31, 33
  substitutes, 44, 45
Chemical analysis and sampling certificates, 117, 118, 132
Chemical industries, 17
Chicago Board of Trade, 65
Chile, 34, 36, 168
China
  information sources, 164, 165, 168, 176, 179, 195, 205–06, 210
  metals monopoly, 70
  strategic metals production, 34, 36, 37, 70, 74, 122
Chrome, 29, 55, 197, 200
Chromite, 16, 56, 70, 167, 170
Chromium, 30, 33, 138, 146, 158
  abundance, 19, 21
  cartel and monopoly effects, 38, 70, 127
  criticality and substitution, 42–46
  ferroalloy metal, 92, 93
  from scrap, 50, 51
  future potential, 89
  information sources, 168, 169, 186, 188, 192–94, 200
  investing in, 89, 92, 93, 143

political vulnerability, 32–35, 96
price, 18, 23, 73, 78, 79
production, 23, 30, 31, 33, 34, 38, 39
trading units and purity level, 99
uses, 8, 11, 14–16, 81, 84
Coal, 155, 156, 196, 197
Cobalt, 24, 56, 129, 138, 158
  abundance, 21
  by-product, 36, 83
  cartel and monopoly effects, 36, 70, 122
  criticality and substitution, 42–47
  from scrap, 49–51
  future potential, 89
  imports, 30, 33, 83
  information sources, 167–70, 172, 173, 186, 192–95, 200
  investing in, 89, 92, 93, 143
  political vulnerability, 32–35, 96
  price, 18, 23, 26–27, 73, 78, 122–24, 126, 141
  production, 23, 30–34, 38, 39
  stockpiling, 55
  superalloy metal, 92, 93
  trading units and purity level, 99
  uses, 8, 14, 15, 17, 42, 46, 49, 81
Cobalt Development Institute, 36, 42, 122, 173
Cobalt Information Center, 173
Colombia, 29
Columbium, 138, 158
  abundance, 21
  by-product, 36–37
  cartel, 38
  criticality and substitution, 43–45
  ferroalloy and superalloy metal, 92, 93
  from scrap, 50, 51
  information sources, 169, 170, 186, 193, 194, 197, 200
  investing in, 92, 93
  political vulnerability, 96
  price, 18, 27, 73, 123

220

INDEX

Columbium (*continued*)
 production, 29–31, 33, 34, 39
 stockpiling, 55
 trading units and purity level, 99
 uses, 8, 13, 14
Comark Commodities, 144
Comark World Metals Fund, 134, 144
Commerce Department (US), 165–66
Commodities, 72, 90–91, 136
 broker, 90–91
Commodity Exchange (New York) (COMEX), 65, 90, 139, 143, 176
Commodity Futures Trading Commission (CFTC), 81, 90
Commodity News Services, 75, 76
Communist countries
 expanding steel industry, 92
 mining monopolies, 67, 69–70
Composites, 47–48
Computers, 8–12, 150
Confirmation of purchase, 112–13
Congress (US), 81, 85, 86
Consolidated Durham, 158
Conti Commodities, 65
Copper, 3, 30, 40, 59, 139
 abundance, 19, 21
 by-product dependence, 97, 153
 cartels, 36
 from scrap, 50
 information sources, 168, 172, 173, 177, 193, 196
 investing in, 64, 90
 price, 71, 123, 124
 production, 31, 83, 94
 stock backing, 154, 156
 stockpiling, 55
 substitutes, 44, 45
 uses, 8, 12, 13
Copper Development Association, 173
Copper Development Institute, 12
Copper Exporting Countries, Intergovernmental Council of, 36, 177

Corporations
 reports and research, 183–84
 stock investments, 153–59
Criticality, 28–40
 and substitution, 41–48
Cuba, 4, 69, 70, 164, 168–69, 177
Czechoslovakia, 69

Diamonds, 36, 142, 197
Documents relation to strategic metals, 112–20
 arbitration agreement, 119
 assay certificate, 117–18, 128
 client trust account, 113
 confirmation of purchase, 112–13
 risk statements, 118–19
 storage and insurance, 116–17, 128
 transfer on sale, 128, 152
 warehouse receipts or warrants, 113–15, 128
Drexel, Burmham, Lambert, Inc., 65

Eagle-Pitcher, 158
Electronic Industries Association, 9
Electronics industry, 8–13, 92, 94, 95
Electronics metals, 4, 9–11, 40
 investing in, 94, 101, 118, 139
 metals included, 92
 scrap, 52–53
Electo-optics metals
 investing in, 92, 94, 101, 118
 metals included, 93
Energy resources and costs, 11, 74, 97, 155
Environment, 16–17, 94, 97–98
 regulation, 83–84
Environmental Protection Agency, 164
Europe, West, 28, 31, 54, 97, 104
 mining investments, 155
 strategic metals imports, 30, 33, 35

Federal Emergency Management Agency, 164
Ferroalloys, 157, 158, 173
 investing in, 64, 92, 93, 96
 metals included, 93
 prices, 78, 79
 processing, 84
 uses, 11, 15–16
Ferroalloys Association, 173
Ferroalloys Producers Association, 173
Ferrochrome, 16, 27, 29
 cartel and monopoly effects, 38, 70
 stockpile funds, 149
Fiber optics, 5, 12–13, 94
Float account, 63
Force majeure, 119
Foreign Broadcast Information Service (FBIS), 164
Forward Looking Infrared (FLIR), 7
France, 32, 34, 37, 54, 56
 information sources, 169, 176, 177, 181, 184
 metal producing companies, 153
 strategic metals stockpiles, 97
Franklin Group, 147
Free market price, 74, 76, 79
Funds; *See* Mutual funds
Futures, 66, 90

Gadolinium, 10
Gallium, 33, 48, 92, 93, 194
 abundance, 21
 by-product, 37
 criticality and substitution, 43–45
 from scrap, 51, 53
 investing in, 92–94
 political vulnerability, 33, 34
 price, 23, 73, 123, 124
 production, 23, 29, 33, 34, 39
 trading units and purity level, 99, 100
 uses, 5, 8, 10–12, 151
Germanium, 48, 92, 93, 139
 abundance, 21
 by-product, 37, 83
 criticality and substitution, 43–45
 from scrap, 51, 53, 126

221

INDEX

Germanium (*continued*)
 information sources, 172, 186, 192–94
 investing in, 92–94, 107, 143
 monopoly effect, 70
 political vulnerability, 32–34
 price, 27, 73, 123, 124, 126
 production, 29, 31, 33, 34, 39, 158
 trading units and purity level, 99, 100
 uses, 5–10, 12, 13, 151
Germany, East, 69
Germany, West, 15, 30, 32, 34, 54, 56, 97, 153, 170
Golconda Investors, 147
Gold, 5, 33, 59, 72, 93, 158
 abundance, 20–22
 by-product, 36, 97
 cartels and monopoly effect, 36, 70
 from scrap, 51
 information sources, 168–70, 172, 174, 186, 188, 196, 197, 200, 201
 investing in, 62, 64, 90
 liquidity, 19
 mutual funds, 135, 139, 146–48, 151–52
 political vulnerability, 32, 33
 price, 23, 71
 and strategic metals, 18–20
 substitutes, 44, 45
 uses, 7, 8, 10, 13
Gold Institute, 174
Government information sources
 international, 166–72
 US, 163–66
Government regulations, 152
Griffiths, Daniel C. & Co., Ltd., 117
Group investments, 91, 107; *See also* Mutual funds

Hafnium, 82
 abundance, 21
 substitutes, 44, 45
 uses, 8, 47
Health and safety regulations, 84–85
Hong Kong and Shanghai Trustee, Ltd., 141
Hong Kong Gold and Silver Exchange, 65

Hong Kong Metals Merchants Association, 177
Hungary, 34, 69
Hutton, E.F., 142

India, 180, 191, 198
Indium, 82, 138
 abundance, 21
 by-product, 37, 83
 criticality and substitution, 43–45
 electro-optics metal, 93
 from scrap, 51, 53
 information sources, 168, 191–94, 200
 investing in, 94, 143
 monopoly effect, 70
 political vulnerability, 34
 price, 18, 23, 27, 73, 123, 124
 production, 23, 30, 34, 39
 trading units and purity level, 99
 uses, 5–9, 11, 13, 151
Indonesia, 36
Inflation, 18, 24, 25, 64, 74, 125, 135, 148
 price adjustments for, 20, 67
Information sources, 73, 75–79, 162–218
 books on strategic metals, 201–04
 business and trade publications, 205–07
 conferences, seminars, and symposia, 181–83
 corporate public relations, 183–84
 geopolitical publications, 207–12
 independent research organizations, 188–90
 international government sources, 166–72
 metal industry publications, 190–96
 metal industry statistics and directories, 185–88
 metal trade organizations, 176–78
 metals recycling organizations, 184–85
 military publications, 212–15
 mining industry publications, 196–201

professional metals societies, 178–81
strategic metals prices, 73
strategic metals producers associations, 172–75
technology publications, 215–18
US government sources, 163–66
Insurance, 91, 113, 115–17, 128, 132, 152
Interactive Data Corporation, 78
Interest rates, 98
Intergovernmental Council of Copper Exporting Countries (CIPEC), 36, 177
International Association of Tungsten Producers, 37
International Investors, Inc., 147
International Lead and Zinc Study Group, 37
International Magnesium Association, 174
International Mercury Producers Association (ASIMER), 37
International Precious Metals Institute (IPMI), 174
International Tin Council, 36, 177
International trade, 30, 31, 65, 71
 import and export duties, 82–83, 116
Investing in strategic metals, 20, 22, 24–27, 58–70, 88–111, 159
 assets necessary, 88–90
 choosing metals, 91–94
 diversification, 24
 documents, 112–20
 group investments, 91, 107
 how to buy, 88–111
 information sources, 162–218
 metal company stocks, 153–59
 minimum units and metal purity, 98–101
 mutual funds, 134–52
 price information, 71–79
 quality and price, 98–101, 108, 109
 risk, 20, 22, 24

222

INDEX

Investing (continued)
  role of metals broker, 58, 63, 101–19, 128–31, 136, 137
  selection criteria, 94–98
  when to buy, 124, 125
  when to sell, 107–08, 121–32
Investment seminars, 181–82
Iridium, 33, 93, 146
  cartel and monopoly effects, 38, 70
  future potential, 89
  information sources, 191–94, 201
  investing in, 89, 94, 143, 159
  political vulnerability, 32–35, 159
  price, 23, 73
  production, 23, 29, 33, 34, 39
  scarcity, 19–20, 22
  stockpiling, 55
  trading units and purity level, 99
  uses, 5, 10, 13, 35
Iron, 3, 59, 64, 72, 156
  ore, 30, 196
  and steel industry, 16, 77
  substitutes, 44–46
Isle of Man, tax laws, 140
Italy, 56, 77, 97, 179, 198

Japan, 16, 28, 30–32, 77, 104, 180, 206
  aerospace industry, 14–15
  electronics industry, 11
  strategic metals production, 34
  strategic metals stockpiles, 54, 97, 149
Johannesburg Stock Exchange, 144
Johns-Manville, 158
Joint Chiefs of Staff (US), 164–65

Korea, North, 69
Korea, South, 56

Ladish Co., 157
Laser weapons, 4–6, 94
Latin America, 67, 155, 199, 200
Laws affecting strategic metals, 80–86

Lead, 3, 8, 30, 59, 64, 71, 90, 94, 139
  by-product dependence, 97, 153
  information sources, 175, 193, 196
  stock backing, 154, 156
  stockpiling, 55
  substitutes, 44
  toxicity, 84
Leigh and Sillavan Ltd., 141
Lexington Goldfund, 147
Library of Congress (US), 165
Light metals, uses, 4–8
Liquidity, 19, 22, 27, 61, 91, 136, 150, 151
Lithium, 13, 73, 158
  abundance, 21
  criticality and substitution, 43
  from scrap, 51
  information sources, 170, 186, 193, 194
  production, 30, 39
  trading units and purity level, 99
Lloyd's of London, 91, 116
Loans, collateral for, 132
Lobbying associations, 22
London Metals Exchange, 65, 90, 113, 114, 116, 118, 139, 141, 143, 177, 198

Magnesium, 96, 138
  abundance, 21
  criticality and substitution, 43–46
  from scrap, 50, 51
  information sources, 168–70, 172, 173, 186, 191–94, 200, 201
  instability, 118
  price, 18, 23, 27, 73, 123, 124
  production, 23, 30, 38, 39
  trading units and purity level, 99
  uses, 6, 17
Magnesium Association, International, 174
Malaysia, 34, 36
Manganese, 146
  abundance, 21
  cartel, 38
  criticality and substitution, 42–45
  ferroalloy metal, 92, 93

from scrap, 51
  information sources, 169, 170, 172, 174, 186, 188, 191–94, 197, 200
  investing in, 92, 93, 143
  political vulnerability, 32–35, 96
  price, 27, 73, 78
  production, 30, 31, 33, 34, 38, 39
  stockpiling, 55
  trading units and purity level, 99
  uses, 15–17, 84
Manganese Center, 174
Mauretania, 36
McDonnell-Douglas Automation, 150
McGraw-Hill, 77, 194, 195
MEMACO (Zambia), 68
Mercury, 73, 143
  abundance, 21
  cartel, 37
  information sources, 168–70, 172, 186, 188, 191–94, 200
  political vulnerability, 33, 34
  production, 33, 34, 39
  stockpiling, 55
  substitutes, 44, 45
  toxicity, 84
  trading units and purity level, 99
Metal industry, information sources, 185–88, 190–96
Metal Powder Industries Association, 174
Metal purity, 99–101
Metal trade organizations, list, 176–78
Metal traders, 58–70, 75, 101, 102, 105, 106, 108, 109, 113, 130, 137–39
Metals broker
  activities, 58–63, 74–75, 101–19, 128–31, 136, 137
  choosing, 101–08
  commission, 62, 63, 106–10, 115
  customer trust account, 104, 106, 113
  documents for investor, 112–15
  and mutual funds, 136, 137
  research backing, 110–11
  selling to, 128–29

223

INDEX

Military publications, list, 212–15
Military uses of strategic metals, 3–17, 92
Mineral Sands Producers Association, 174
Mines, Bureau of (US), 78, 163, 166
Minimum trading units, 98–101
Mining industry, 77, 151
   information sources, 196–201
   investing in, 153–59
   producers, 66–67, 153–59
   state quasi-cartels, 67
Minor Metals Traders Association, 141, 177
Molybdenum, 104–05, 138, 154, 156, 158
   abundance, 21
   cartel, 38
   criticality and substitution, 28, 43–46
   ferroalloy and superalloy metal, 92, 93
   from scrap, 51
   information sources, 169, 170, 172, 186, 188, 191–94, 200, 201
   investing in, 92, 93, 104, 105, 143
   price, 18, 23, 27, 73, 78, 105
   production, 23, 28, 38, 39
   stockpiling, 54, 149
   trading units and purity level, 99
   uses, 13, 14, 16, 17
Money market funds, 135, 139
Mongolia, 69
Monopolies, State operated, 67, 69, 70; *See also* Cartels
Mozambique, 26
Mutual funds, 59–61, 97, 102, 111, 121, 134–52
   Bache Halsey Stuart Metals Fund, 143
   capital requirements, 136
   Comark World Metals, 144
   geopolitically oriented, 145–46
   gold funds, 146–48
   government regulations, 152
   private stockpiling, 149–50
   registration process, 136–37
   South African Minerals Fund, 144–45
   starting your own, 150–52
   Strategic Materials Corporation, 142–43
   Strategic Metals Corporation portfolio, 138
   Strategic Metals Trust, 140–41

Namibia, 70, 146, 171
   germanium from, 29, 31, 34, 119
   uranium from, 37
National Aeronautics and Space Administration (NASA), 46, 47, 50
National Defense Stockpile Inventory (US), 54, 55
National Strategic Defense Stockpile (US), 97, 164
National Technical Information Service (NTIS), 162, 195
Nationalization, 67, 68, 74, 82, 155
Natural gas, 155, 156
Netherlands, 178
New Guinea, 36
New International Economic Order (NIEO), 38, 208
New York Commodity Exchange; *See* Commodity Exchange (New York)
New York Mercantile Exchange, 65, 90, 139, 178
New York Stock Exchange, 147, 157, 158
Nickel, 3, 33, 40, 59, 129, 139, 193
   abundance, 19, 21
   by-product dependence, 97, 153
   ferroalloy metal, 92
   from scrap, 50
   investing in, 64, 90, 92, 93
   price, 71, 123, 124
   production, 33, 94
   stockpiling, 55
   substitutes, 44–46
   uses, 8, 14
Nigeria, 34
Non-ferrous metals, information sources, 174, 175, 185, 187, 195
Nord Resources, 158
Norway, 157, 181
Nuclear industry, 13–14, 92

Occupational Safety and Health Administration (OSHA), 84, 165
Ohio Ferro-Alloys, 157, 158
Oregon Metallurgical Company (Oremet), 156–58
Organization of American States (OAS), 209
Organization of Minerals Exporting Countries (OMEC), xi
Organization of Petroleum Exporting Countries (OPEC), xi, 26, 38, 68, 69, 155
Osmium, 33, 73
   abundance, 21
   criticality and substitution, 43
   information sources, 186, 191, 193, 194, 200
   political vulnerability, 32, 33, 35
   production, 29, 33
   trading units and purity level, 99
Over-the-counter market, 72, 158

Palladium, 139, 146, 158
   abundance, 21
   by-product, 83
   cartel, 38
   catalytic metal, 93, 94
   criticality and substitution, 43
   from scrap, 51
   information sources, 191–94, 200
   investing in, 90, 94, 159
   political vulnerability, 32–35, 193
   price, 71, 73, 78
   production, 29, 31, 33, 34
   stockpiling, 55
   uses, 16, 17, 83
Peat, Marwick, Mitchell & Co., 141
Peru, 36
Petroleum, 17, 94, 155–56, 196
Phibro (metals trader), 65
Philippines, 170
Phillips & Drew, 146
Phosphates, 156

INDEX

Plastics, 47, 48
Platinum, 5, 33, 139, 146, 158
  abundance, 19–20, 22
  by-product, 36, 83
  catalytic metal, 93, 94
  criticality and substitution, 43
  from scrap, 51, 52
  information sources, 168, 191–94, 196, 200, 201
  investing in, 90, 94, 159
  monopoly effect, 70
  political vulnerability, 32–35, 159
  price, 19–20, 23, 71, 73, 78
  production, 23, 29, 31, 33, 34
  stockpiling, 55
  uses, 10, 16, 17, 83
Platinum metals, 31, 35, 38, 39, 49, 96
  criticality and substitution, 44–46
  from scrap, 49–51
  information sources, 168, 171, 186
  political vulnerability, 96
  See also Iridium, Osmium, Rhodium, Ruthenium
Plutonium, 13
Poland, 69, 135
Policy conferences, 181, 182
Political instability, 96, 145–46, 153, 158–59
Potash, 156
Precious Metals Holdings, 147
Precious Metals Trust (UK), 135
Precious Metals Trust PLC, 146
Price (for strategic metals)
  bumps, 122–25
  cartel effects, 35–38
  environmental effects, 83–84
  fixed, 64, 65, 67
  fluctuations, 26, 89, 97, 121, 145
  free market, 74, 76, 79
  government controlled, 28–29, 40, 68
  information sources, 71–79, 106, 166, 190–207
  minimum trading units, 98–101, 108, 109
  producer controlled, 67, 74, 79

and scrap recovery, 50
  stockpile effect, 97
  supply relationship, 20, 22–27, 126, 155
Producers' associations, list, 172–75
Professional meetings, 181–83
Professional metals societies, list, 178–81
Prudential Insurance Company, 65, 102, 143
Purchase order, 112–13, 128

Rare earths, 44, 45, 168
Recycling, 49–53, 95, 98
  list of organizations, 184–85
Refinement International, 52
Refractories Institute, 175
Refractory metals, 92
Research, 109–11, 130–31, 139
  independent organizations, 188–90
Research Capital Fund, 147
Reuters, 75, 76
Rhenium, 129
  abundance, 20, 22
  by-product, 83
  catalytic metal, 93, 94
  criticality and substitution, 43–45
  from scrap, 51, 53
  information sources, 168, 193, 194
  political vulnerability, 34
  price, 23, 27, 73, 123, 124
  production, 23, 30, 34, 39
  trading units and purity level, 99, 100
  uses, 9, 13, 17, 47
Rhodium, 56, 129, 138, 146
  abundance, 19–20, 22
  criticality and substitution, 43
  from scrap, 50
  information sources, 186, 191–94, 200, 201
  investing in, 89, 92–94, 107, 143, 159
  monopoly effect, 70
  political vulnerability, 32–35, 159
  price, 16, 18, 23, 73
  production, 23, 29, 31, 33, 34, 39

trading units and purity level, 99
  uses, 4, 5, 16, 17, 35, 83
Risk
  acceptance form, 118
  disclosure statements, 119
Romania, 69
Rotterdam (strategic metals center), 86, 107, 113–16, 130
Ruthenium, 10, 72, 129
  abundance, 20, 22
  criticality and substitution, 43
  information sources, 186, 191, 193, 194
  investing in, 73, 92–94
  political vulnerability, 32, 33, 35
  production, 29, 31, 33
  trading units and purity level, 99
Rutile, 56

Sampling and weight certificates, 117, 118, 132
Scandium, 30, 31, 33, 44, 45, 51
Scrap metal, recycling, 49–53, 126
Securities and Exchange Commission (SEC), 136, 137, 142, 152
Selenium, 72, 82, 93, 94, 143
  abundance, 21
  by-product, 36, 83
  criticality and substitution, 43–45
  from scrap, 51, 53
  information sources, 168, 175, 188, 191, 193, 194, 200
  price, 23, 73, 122–24
  production, 23, 30, 39
  trading units and purity level, 99
  uses, 5, 7, 8, 11, 17, 151
Selenium-Tellurium Development Association, 175
Selling strategic metals, 108–09, 121–32, 138
Semiconductors, 8–11
Sensors and detectors, 6–7, 94
Shipping costs, 115, 116
Silicon, 48, 138
  abundance, 21

225

INDEX

Silicon (*continued*)
 criticality and substitution, 43–45
 from scrap, 51
 information sources, 168, 169, 186, 191, 193, 194
 investing in, 92–94
 price, 18, 73, 123, 124
 production value, 38, 39
 trading units and purity level, 99
 uses, 5, 7–9, 11, 15–17, 47
Silver, 4, 20, 154, 156, 158
 abundance, 21
 by-product, 36
 from scrap, 51, 52
 information sources, 169, 170, 172, 175, 186, 188, 191–94, 197, 200, 201
 investing in, 90
 price, 23, 71, 73
 stockpiling, 56
 substitutes, 44, 45
 uses, 10, 13
Silver Institute, 175
Sinclair Group, 102, 142
Solar power cell, 11, 151
South Africa, 52, 127, 153
 foreign investments in, 144, 145, 153, 159
 gold cartel, 36
 gold trust funds, 147, 148
 information sources, 170–71, 173, 175, 177, 178, 180, 197, 204, 206–07, 211, 212
 mining stocks, 158–59
 political instability, 69, 146, 152, 158–59
 strategic metals from, 4, 16, 25, 29, 31–38, 82, 122, 135, 149, 157
South African Strategic Minerals Fund, 135, 144–45
Southern Africa, 32–38, 46, 127, 197, 211
Soviet Union, 83, 135
 gold cartel, 36
 information sources, 164, 165, 171–72, 176, 196, 204, 207, 211, 215
 military weapons, 3–4, 6, 11–13
 state metals monopoly, 69, 70
 strategic metals production, 29, 31–38, 74, 122

strategic metals stockpile, 56
SOZACOM (Zaire), 68
Space technology, 3–6, 15
Spain, 56, 97, 181
State cartels and monopolies, 67–70
State Department (US), 166
Steel, 3, 11, 12, 64, 72
 industry, 16, 27, 50, 92
 Stockpiling, 54–57, 85, 95, 97
 private funding, 149–50
Strategic Investments Fund, 148
Strategic Materials Corporation, 135
Strategic Metals & Critical Materials, Inc., 102, 142–43
Strategic Metals Corporation, 62, 102, 108
 managed portfolio, 135, 138–40
Strategic Metal Trust, 135, 140–41
Strategic Stockpile Corporation, 149
Strontium, 17, 21, 30, 31, 33, 39, 50, 51
Substitution, 41–48, 95–96, 126, 130, 131, 150
Superalloys, 14, 47, 92, 93
Sweden, 56, 97
Switzerland, 29, 179
Synthetic materials, 46–48

Tantalum, 101, 138, 158
 abundance, 21
 by-product, 36–37
 criticality and substitution, 43–46
 ferroalloy metal, 92, 93
 fraudulent sales, 80
 from scrap, 50, 51, 53
 information sources, 167, 169, 171, 175, 186, 191, 193, 194, 197
 political vulnerability, 33, 34, 96
 price, 18, 23, 27, 73, 79, 123, 124
 production, 23, 31–34, 39
 stockpiling, 55
 trading units and purity level, 99
 uses, 8–10, 12, 14

Tantalum Producers Association, 175
Tantalum Producers International Study Center, 175
Taxation, 81, 82, 85, 98, 132
Technology, 3–6, 15, 151
 publications, 215–18
Technology Assessment, Office of, 165
Teck Corporation, 158
Telecommunications, 12–13, 94
Teledyne Corporation, 158
Tellurium, 143
 by-product, 36, 83
 from scrap, 51, 53
 information sources, 168, 175, 186, 188, 191, 193, 194, 200
 price, 23, 27, 73, 124
 production, 23, 30, 39
 substitutes, 44, 45
 trading units and purity level, 99
 uses, 5, 7, 8, 11, 151
Thailand, 34, 36
Thallium
 abundance, 21
 by-product, 36, 83
 from scrap, 50, 51
 substitutes, 44, 45
 toxicity, 84
 uses, 13, 17
Third World, 15, 16, 26, 74, 82, 96
 New International Economic Order, 38
 political instability, 153, 154
 steel industry, 92
 strategic metals, 30, 82
Thorium, 13, 21, 30, 33, 43, 51, 55, 73, 192
Tin, 3, 17, 30, 33, 90, 139, 153
 abundance, 21
 cartels and monopoly effect, 36–37, 70
 from scrap, 51
 information sources, 168–70, 172, 177, 186, 188, 197, 200, 201
 prices, 27, 71, 78
 production, 31, 70
 stockpiling, 55
 substitution, 44, 45
Tin Council, International, 36, 177

226

INDEX

Titanium
  abundance, 21
  cartel and monopoly effect, 37–38, 70
  criticality and substitution, 43–45
  from scrap, 50, 51
  information sources, 167–70, 172, 174, 186, 188, 192–95, 197, 200
  investing in, 92, 93, 143
  price, 27, 73, 78, 122–24
  production, 30, 33, 34, 37–39, 156, 158, 167
  stockpiling, 55
  trading units and purity level, 99
  uses, 6, 8, 14, 16, 17, 47, 81, 92, 93
Titanium Association (Japan), 174
Toronto Stock Exchange, 158
Treasury Department (US), 166
Tungsten, 138, 158
  abundance, 21
  cartel and monopoly effect, 37, 70
  criticality and substitution, 43–45
  ferroalloy and superalloy metal, 92, 93
  from scrap, 50, 51
  information sources, 168–70, 172, 175, 186, 188, 191–94, 200, 201
  political vulnerability, 33, 34, 96
  price, 18, 23, 27, 73, 78, 123, 124
  production, 23, 33, 34, 38, 39, 70
  stockpiling, 55
  trading units and purity level, 99
  uses, 8, 13, 14, 47
Tungsten Association, Primary, 175

United Kingdom, 34, 37, 56, 97, 153
  information sources, 177, 180, 184, 193, 198, 200
United Nations, 37, 38, 135
United Services Fund, 148

United States
  ban on uranium imports, 37
  customs duties, 82–83
  defense policy, 81
  strategic metals fund, 142–43
  strategic metals imports, 24, 32, 33, 35, 82–83
  strategic metals production, 28–31, 34, 36–38, 153–55
  strategic metals stockpiles, 19, 54–56, 97, 164
  warehouses, 83, 115, 116
  weapons systems, 3–4, 6, 12
Uranium, 13, 59, 73
  abundance, 21
  cartel, 37
  criticality and substitution, 43
  information sources, 169, 171, 175, 186, 188, 191, 193, 197
  oil companies interest in, 155
  political vulnerability, 32, 33
Uranium Institute, 175

Vanadium, 51
  abundance, 21
  cartel, 38
  criticality and substitution, 43
  ferroalloy metal, 16, 92, 93
  information sources, 169, 170, 186, 188, 192–94, 200, 201
  investing in, 92, 93, 143
  political vulnerability, 32–35, 96
  price, 23, 27, 73, 89
  production, 23, 29, 30, 39
  stockpiling, 55
  trading units and purity level, 99
  uses, 8, 13, 16, 17
Vancouver Stock Exchange, 157–58
Vietnam, 4, 69

Warehousing, 83, 85, 86, 91, 107, 114–16
  costs, 114, 118, 152

receipt (warrant), 62, 91, 104–08, 113–15, 128, 132, 152
selection criteria, 95, 96
World Bureau of Metal Statistics, 187–88

Ytterbium, 21
Yttrium, 21, 33, 44, 45, 72
Yugoslavia, 36, 69, 70

Zaire, 24, 32, 127
  cartel and government monopoly, 36, 68
  cobalt production, 26, 34, 68, 122
  germanium production, 29, 31, 34
  information sources, 172, 178
Zambia, 127
  cartel and government monopoly, 36, 68, 70
  cobalt production, 26, 31, 34
  tantalum reserves, 32
Zimbabwe, 29, 127, 146, 167, 200
  metals production, 16, 34, 70, 126
Zinc, 3, 8, 29, 30, 33, 40, 59, 64, 90, 139, 158
  availability, 19, 21
  by-products, 37, 83, 97, 153
  cartel, 37
  information sources, 175, 193, 196
  price, 71, 124
  production, 83, 84, 94
  stock backing, 154, 156
  stockpiling, 55
  substitutes, 44, 45
Zinc Institute, 175
Zirconium, 33, 158
  abundance, 21
  criticality and substitution, 43–45
  from scrap, 51
  information sources, 169, 170, 174, 186, 191–94, 200
  price, 27, 73, 123, 124
  production, 30, 39
  trading units and purity level, 99
  uses, 8, 13

227

Communications